Katrina

and the Forgotten Gulf Coast

To Ann + Jim Enjoy Betty Plombon 2007

by
Betty Plombon

First published by Dog Ear Publishing
4010 W. 86th Street, Ste H
Indianapolis, IN 46268
www.dogearpublishing.net

ISBN: 1-59858-220-8

This book is printed on acid-free paper.

Printed in the United States of America

Acknowlegements

I am very grateful to:

Linda Baur, who inspired me to begin this book and later refused to allow me to drop the project when I became overwhelmed with the struggles of life.

Doris Wunderlik, who spent so many hours proof reading, correcting and advising me on valuable details.

Those who graciously allowed to be interviewed, who pushed aside their emotions and shared their memories for you to read.

Those who shared their photos to use in this book.

Table of Contents

Introduction Page

It was the worst natural disaster in U.S. history. Katrina arrived on the Mississippi Gulf Coast on August 29, 2005, and she will never be forgotten!

While other storms may pack greater wind speeds, Katrina pushed the largest surge ever recorded on earth and the most cataclysmic, widespread storm to strike the mainland of the United States. It hit the Mississippi Coast dead-on.

I will attempt to describe the days around Katrina and August 29, 2005, and what happened in the small, unincorporated golf resort town of Diamondhead, Mississippi, and her neighboring communities. As the media reported on Katrina, Diamondhead was seldom mentioned in the news because it is not an incorporated entity, but is a part of Hancock County.

You have to be in South Mississippi and see it for yourself to comprehend the utter destruction that looks much like that of Berlin or Hiroshima after World War II. It is impossible to grasp the disaster as a whole from afar. A television can display only a single screen of the damage at one time; until you have driven mile after mind-numbing mile and view the complete nothingness where cities, homes and businesses once stood, only then can you begin to understand the scope of what happened here in South Mississippi.

No photograph or words can capture the enormity and destruction of Katrina's fury. To actually see it is the only way to visualize the scale of this catastrophe. The destruction spreads through many states and over many counties within each state and stretches along the entire shoreline of Mississippi and then inland for miles. Not until you have seen at eye level the destruction and ruins that spread for mile after mile do you realize what Katrina did to South Mississippi.

As you drive around the South, it soon becomes tiring to be viewing so much devastation because it is so widespread and so utterly depressing! One soon begins to want to shut it all out and move on. This is what many choose to do, just move on to another part of the country and not have to go through this ordeal one more time.

People have given conflicting memories of events of that day, probably from stress, but I will tell it as it was related to me.

Author, Betty Plombon

Diamondhead, MS

Diamondhead, MS

Diamondhead is a small, mostly unknown, private residential community, thirty miles west of Biloxi, Mississippi. Malcolm Purcell McLean, entrepreneur and real estate developer, finalized his dream community in 1970. His plans were to capture retired people as they made their way to Florida from New Orleans for vacations. After Camille took away their playgrounds near Biloxi, New Orleaneans began to escape to Florida's emerald shores. Diamondhead consists of 6,400 acres, spread over 10 square miles and is located in Hancock County. It straddles Interstate Hwy 10, as some of the town is located south of the Hwy with most of it to the north. After McLean fought hard for an overhead Interchange off I-10, "Paradise" came alive for the developers as a lavishly marketed, high-elevation resort with golf, tennis, condominiums and inexpensive land for homes.

Diamondhead was designed as a Hawaiian paradise, with streets bearing Hawaiian names and the Yacht Club, Country Club, and Pro Shop resembling Hawaiian buildings. It sits among thousands of pine trees and is a bird and animal refuge. Wonderful gourmet dishes, advertised as "out of this world," have satisfied those who dropped into the Country Club or Yacht Club. The area has been nicknamed, "A Little Bit of Paradise."

With 11 miles of coastline, the community is surrounded on three sides by water, the Bay of St. Louis on the south, the Jourdan River on the west and the Bayou Benesheewa/Rotten Bayou on the north edge. Diamondhead ranges from 4 feet above sea level to 85 feet at its highest point. In 1999, the local newspaper, *The Diamondhead News,* told us: "We are fortunate here in Diamondhead, as we are on high ground."

The Diamondhead community now claims more than 8,000 inhabitants, about 3,600 homes and is still unincorporated. It is operated

by a Board of Directors representing the Property Owners Association
or POA, instead of a mayor-council. Thirty-five years after it began,
Diamondhead consists of mostly working families. The John C. Stennis
Space Center is located very close to Diamondhead. It is here that the
Apollo rocket engines were first fired. About 4,500 people, many in the
science and engineering fields, live in Diamondhead. The slogan, "If
you want to go to the moon, you first have to go through Hancock
County, Mississippi," was circulated to promote the area.

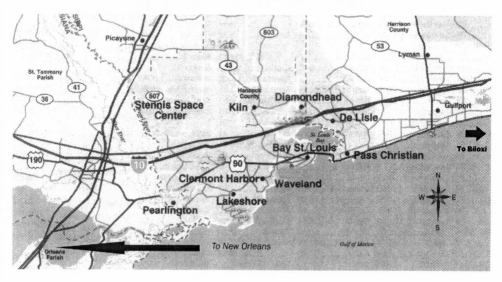

Storm Surge and Hurricanes

A storm surge is simply the ocean's surface, pushed towards shore by the force of wind swirling around a tropical storm. It is associated with low pressure and persistent wind over a shallow body of water. High wind causes the water to pile up above normal sea level. Highest waters are always in the right front quadrant of where the winds are the strongest. In deeper waters, high water can be dispersed down and away from the storm.

High water of a hurricane begins days before the storm hits land. Water is heavy and very slow to move when it is being pushed. Water rises beneath a hurricane for two reasons: The low air pressure creates a vacuum that sucks the water upwards and the wind moving in a counterclockwise, inward direction is pushing and gathering water toward the front of the eye of the storm.

When the storm enters a coastal shallow, the bulge drags against the sea floor, slowing its forward motion, and the faster-moving tail end of the swell piles up and over the front end, increasing the height of the surge. Meanwhile, the normal storm waves are still on top of the surface. The Mississippi coastline has long stretches of shallow water depths, making it very vulnerable to storm surges. The level of a surge is also determined by the slope of the continental shelf with a shallow rise allowing a greater surge to rush onto the land, going inland for many miles.

A Category 4 storm can have a much larger surge than a Category 5 storm if it is slow and large in size, as it was in Katrina. All conditions on August 29, 2005, were right for "the perfect storm."

1. Wind strength of 120 to 145 MPH causing higher waves (During the tornadoes: 150 to 175)
2. Low air pressure of 27.17 inches on the 29th but 26.64 the day before
3. Size of the eye (Katrina was 32 miles wide when a normal Category 4 storm has a width of 10 miles)
4. Distance the winds extend from center (125 miles from center compared to 60 miles in Camille)
5. Speed it comes ashore (this was a slow moving storm)
6. The angle when it hit was directly from the south
7. High Tide
8. A shallow offshore shelf

Katrina was listed as a Hurricane Category 5 the day before it reached land. Even though the wind slowed to a Category 3 at landfall, the surge still reflected Category 5 conditions because the surge was slower to change and slow down. The inner eyewall weakened before landfall while the winds became stronger 30–50 miles east of the center, especially above the surface of the water. The winds were spreading out and the storm remained unusually large. The winds found near the eyewall determine the official strength in terms of category and Katrina was downgraded to a Category 3 at landfall. However, the barometric pressure remained at a strong Category 4 or 5 intensity. The Weather Bureau was right in categorizing Katrina as a size 3, but horribly wrong about its strength, which equaled a Category 5 storm. Bands of intense currents of air, both in the eyewall and in rain bands outside the eye, brought strong winds aloft down to the ground in fierce gusts, triggering scattered tornadoes and downbursts. Severe damage resulted from these gusts prior to the final landfall.[1]

The Louisiana coastline, which extends 120 miles into the Gulf, began to funnel the mass of water being pushed by Katrina towards Mississippi. For two days, the storm moved at a right angle toward the coast, which made the water go higher, like snow in front of a shovel moving in a straight line. The natural waters off the coastline gave the storm water very little space to dissipate.

The shallow bays at each end of Harrison County amplified the surge by funneling water into a small space, which is why the highest storm-surge values were in the Bay of St. Louis.

The surge rose rapidly one to two hours before the final landfall at the mouth of the Pearl River and peaked within an hour or so after that.

During Katrina, Waveland, which is only a few feet above sea level, was hit by a 35-foot storm surge; a surge of at least 15 feet deluged the entire Mississippi coast. Lands never before flooded were covered in water. The surge pushed water to 28–30 feet high at the intersection of Hwy 10 and 603, which is almost seven miles north of the Gulf of Mexico. The Kiln, or "The Kiln," (pronounced "Kill") north and west of Diamondhead, and ten miles north of the Gulf Coast, saw at least 30 feet of floodwater. The surge began about 8 a.m. along the western part of the Mississippi coast and about 9 a.m. along the eastern coast. It peaked from 10 a.m. to 11 a.m. and began to recede about 12 noon.

These times and heights were hard to reconstruct as all storm surge measuring sites failed well before the height of the storm. Numerous other sources had to be used such as Stennis Space Center professionals, Louisiana Doppler radars and many individual eyewitness reports.

On top of the bulging force of water were waves, and these waves combined with the surge were a very destructive force. As the waves on top of the bulge began crashing into structures, they caused the buildings to collapse and any people within were left to the elements.

Hurricanes generate tornadoes, tightly wound vortices, which arise when adjacent bands of the storm acquire different speeds. These tornadoes snap off utility poles and uproot trees along with removing roofs from buildings. Tornadoes are most common in the right front quadrant of the storm and near the hurricane core within 60 miles of the eye of the storm. Large hurricanes produce more tornadoes than small storms. Because of the size of the storm, locations throughout the coast were exposed to hurricane-force wind gusts for many hours. The author comes from "Tornado Alley," Wisconsin, where tornadoes reduce buildings to rubble with winds of 120–145 miles per hour, lasting only a few moments. A hurricane like Katrina, with the same winds, lasting from 12–14 hours, would surely take down buildings before the water arrived.

The eye of a hurricane, according to those who have witnessed being in one, is eerie. When one occurs during nighttime, the sky will be dark all around, except for one circle showing bright stars. Within twenty minutes the winds will begin blowing again, but coming from the opposite direction. What the first pass of the storm does not take down, it will probably finish off on the second pass.

Even though parts of Diamondhead are more than 70 feet above sea level, water backed up into the surrounding rivers and bayous, flowing over the banks and into homes. Diamondhead did not suffer from Katrina's initial surge of water, but from the gradually rising sea, as continuous hours of high winds pushed the water further and further inland and up the banks of rivers and bayous.

Yacht Club (Photo by Baur)

The Angry Sea

Katrina swung through South Florida on Friday, August 26, as a Category 1 hurricane and soon entered the warm waters of the Gulf of Mexico, not sure of what direction she wanted to take, but gaining power as she moved towards Louisiana and Mississippi.

Sunday, August 28th, was a lovely day to be in South Mississippi, with the clouds sucked away into Katrina. Picture the lovely Gulf of Mexico on a peaceful day, a gentle, flat, sun-speckled bay of water with gentle waves lapping your feet as you wade into it. The ocean breezes warm your body on the white sand beach that extends for miles in either direction. A dramatic sky forms as the sun goes down with spectacular colors. This is known as the "calm before the storm."

However, Katrina is lurking out in the Gulf of Mexico, 200 miles from the Coast and moving closer to land with each hour. She has winds of 172 miles per hour and is now a Category 5 hurricane, but has still not decided where she will strike. Conditions are perfect for a catastrophic storm and mandatory evacuations are soon issued. Millions of residents along the coast grab what they can, load it into cars and begin jamming highways as they leave for areas to the west, north or east. Gas is hard to find, lines are long, some stations already out of gas. There are very few motel vacancies and people must travel far for any room at all, the price of which is highly inflated. Shrimp boats and small yachts are seen leaving the vulnerable harbors, hoping to find a safer haven.

Many would never return to live here again, and would soon regret leaving some of their valuables behind.

Rain began falling around 7 p.m. Sunday night and the swirling winds were picking up and beginning their mournful howl, which would continue for hours. Shortly after midnight, Katrina turned northward toward the Mississippi Delta. By 4 a.m., the next morning the surge began pounding beaches with an unbelievable force. The storm hit south Louisiana at 6:10 a.m., then turned slightly east as she continued her murderous path. On Monday, August 29th, Katrina, the largest U.S. natural disaster on record, slammed into South Mississippi as a Category 4 hurricane, with an angry storm surge up to 35 feet high. The wind gusts were about 143 miles per hour.

The storm surge, which hit between 8–10 a.m., was the highest and most violent surge ever to hit South Mississippi, according to the experts. At 9:45 a.m., the eye of Katrina was making its second landfall near the mouth of the Pearl River on the Louisiana-Mississippi border.

At 10:15, Diamondhead was reported to be on the east side of the eye of Katrina. The eye alone was 30 miles wide and hurricane winds extended for 200 miles inland and 200 miles along the coast.

Residents who stayed were convinced that they would die. In many homes, they clung to anything stationary while their lifelong possessions floated out broken windows. When the water continued to rise, many climbed out those same windows, hoping to swim for safety. They grabbed floating debris or climbed onto treetops, holding on for hours while the terrific winds battered them. Others moved to second stories or attics, huddling together and praying for mercy as the storm howled unmercifully. Some said that the sound, oh the sound, howled like some mythical creature roaring with the voice of a thousand banshees. When it seemed it could not get any worse, the intensity continued to grow even stronger.

The eye of Katrina

Many prayers were said that day, many were answered, some were not.

After 12 hours of wind, six of them severe, Katrina had torn apart communities and destroyed buildings that were hundreds of years old. Thousands of businesses, homes and historical landmarks would never rise from the waters. In shambles and ruin were dozens of schools, bridges, highways, ports, railroads and water and sewer systems. Katrina created the country's biggest refugee crisis in New Orleans, demolished most of the Gulf Coast's historic cities and shattered millions of lives.

Winds of over one hundred miles per hour turned wreckage into lethal weapons. Bricks, broken boards, roof slates, tree limbs, sections of signs and large pieces of metal buildings flew through the air damaging anything in the way. Homes torn from their piers by wind and high water smashed into other buildings, swung around and crashed again into neighbor's homes, creating more destruction. Debris formed mountains that, pushed by the storm surge, moved relentlessly inland destroying everything in its path. Tornadoes formed, snapping power poles, uprooting trees and rupturing roofs; homes that had remained dry from floodwater were soon filled with sodden insulation as their roofs blew off.

As buildings broke up from the wind and water, the screeching of nails pulling loose from studs and joists added another frightening sound to the incessant howling of the wind. When low air pressure outside assaults the higher pressure trapped inside a building, without warning the building may explode sending splintered boards flying through the air.

At full blast a hurricane sounds like a freight train roaring past at full speed and only a few inches away. The first European to survive such force was Christopher Columbus on his second voyage to America in 1495, when a powerful storm sunk two of his three galleons.

Everyone along the coast had been warned throughout the previous weekend that the storm could prove to be even more catastrophic than Camille was and that everyone should evacuate. Those that chose to remain were told that rescuers would not be out at the height of the storm and at risk for their own lives.

Many 911 calls came in to emergency centers; people screamed and begged for help. In Biloxi, police dispatchers received 242 gut-wrenching cries for help where police personnel were spread too thin to conduct door-to-door checks before the storm. It was now too late. Each was told that help could not arrive for several hours. About 9 a.m., several officers did venture out into the storm and brought back about 75 people and 1 dog. After that, the storm was too bad for them to leave their security until the winds died down.

People thrown into the swirling waters were completely helpless unless they managed to hang onto something secure, such as a tree. One cubic yard of water weighs 1,700 pounds, which makes a wave a powerful force. This force can toss a body high in the air or forward for miles. When two-by-fours and beams are continuously slamming a body, weariness and stress soon causes the person to give up or to lose consciousness.

At 12:15 p.m., the storm reversed as the eye passed the Diamondhead area and then the winds began blowing from the southwest. People felt their ears pop as the pressure changed radically. Those sheltering in broken homes surrounded by high water watched as remaining small objects and furniture were drawn quickly to the outside by waters that had begun to recede. By 2:00 p.m., the winds finally dropped below hurricane level. Survivors began wading outside, climbing over rubble to survey the devastation. They began searching for their pets and possessions and to seek or offer help to others.

The monster storm dumped eight to ten inches of rain, with water surges of 34 feet in some places, and devastated nearly 90,000 square miles of central Gulf Coast. Katrina was immediately dubbed by Camille survivors as her "Evil Daughter." In 1969, Camille had made almost the same landfall that Katrina would 37 years later. A Category 5 hurricane, Camille was stronger than her daughter, Katrina, but blew over quickly, hitting only a portion of the coast now devastated by Katrina. What Katrina lacked in wind speed, she more than made up for in storm surge, duration and breadth. For Katrina survivors, the days before Katrina will be fondly remembered as "post-Camille." Moreover, the days after August 29, 2006 will be known as "post-Katrina."

Katrina was not particular in the class of people that she decimated; as she rolled inland for miles, she ruined people with "big houses" and people with "little houses." Some were U.S. Senators, bankers, retired people, but many were of the working class, most of whom were heavily mortgaged. It was a storm that made grown men cry.

Katrina was not just another hurricane. She became the worst national disaster in the history of the nation. Ruination stretches nearly

200 miles from Mobile across all of Mississippi and to the other side of New Orleans. Over a million people were displaced throughout the U.S. Hardest hit, with nearly everything wiped away by Katrina, were Waveland, Bay St. Louis and Pass Christian. These towns were demolished to concrete foundations, buildings crumpled like tinker toys or gutted, leaving only a shell. Critical bridges along Hwy 90 were washed away. Huge damage occurred at Slidell, Pearlington, Long Beach, Gulfport, Biloxi, Ocean Springs and Diamondhead. It was estimated that there was 12.1 billion dollars in damage in Mississippi. Today, Katrina is rated as the storm of all storms.

On Saturday morning, Hancock County Emergency personnel and Diamondhead staff still felt that Katrina would not pose major problems for the community. However, Chip Marz, POA (Property Owners Association) Manager, gathered his "crew" to make sure everything was organized in case Katrina changed course. "We had a plan," said Chip. Heavy road equipment, tractors, front-end loaders, etc. were dispersed around Diamondhead, ready for action at all points. It was not until later in the evening that a mandatory evacuation was declared. Diamondhead Department Heads were called to alert, but soon left again to prepare their own homes.

On Sunday, Katrina took a turn and looked as though she could create problems with high winds. Still, the crew was not at all concerned about high water. Heck! Diamondhead had never been flooded by any storm before. A Command Post was set up at the Country Club. Twenty-six people, including Darrel Kinchin, Chip Marz and wife, staff people, security people, board members and families, stayed there Sunday night. The storm was still shifting and forecasters had still not pinpointed the direct strike area. Later that evening, the cable company shut down service and the phones went out. This Command Post now had no way to receive, communicate or distribute the latest information. They were left with only a battery radio and a small portable TV that received only one station.

Below is an account of the storm on Monday, August 29, 2005, by Chip Marz, Diamondhead General Manager.

On Monday morning about 5:30 a.m., the wind was screeching and screaming and strong enough making it impossible to go outdoors, even in vehicles. Trees were toppling and the rain was being driven sideways.

At 7 a.m., parts of the roof of the Country Club had blown away and about 8 a.m., the electricity went out. No problem, we just turned on the generator. Now, we had power for a few lights, the TV and computer, but no cable service.

The wind kept getting stronger and more awesome and we watched the massive oak trees in the front circle, already naked of their leaves, whipping the branches back and forth, tangling with other branches and bending to the ground.

Water rising fast in the Oaks as seen through the rain and a window. (Photo by Baur)

A section of the roof over the 19-hole grill area gave way and collapsed into the bar. A huge beam blew through the wall. Fortunately, the command center had already moved from this area into the kitchen and when this area began to leak, we moved to the center hallway near the banquet room (we had determined that hallways and the bathrooms were probably the sturdiest part of the Club). Doors were rattling and had to be secured. At some point, we heard a crash and looked into the ballroom. Another portion of the roof had peeled away and water was pouring in from the center section ceiling, filling the glass bowls of the chandelier and drenching everything. We could look up through the ceiling and see the sky.

Now it was really getting scary. It was so dark throughout the building that we frequently had to count off to make sure all 26 of us were still together. In the fear of the moment, we could not even count properly and sometimes we had to count three or four times to get it right. It appeared to be nighttime, even thought it was only mid morning. We had lost water pressure, so the toilets were becoming rather nasty with 26 scared people using them.

With the wind coming in from above, it threatened to blow in the ballroom doors leading into the hallway, where we had made our last stand. Things were looking more and more serious. What would 26 people do if we had to go out into the storm?

At one point, I remember feeling my ears pop and the air mattress I was sitting on start to go blump, blump, blump, which meant low air pressure. All I could think of was tornado, and I yelled, "Bathrooms, now!" Twenty-six people huddled together on the floor of the stinking bathroom.

We kept waiting for the eye of the storm to arrive. We expected it would come right over us, and we needed to use the calm to survey the Club's stability and that of the cart shed, in case we had to abandon the Clubhouse. However, the eye never came; we must have been on the innermost eastern wall without actually being in the eye! We were able to observe the wind shift from the east, to the south, and finally from out of the west as the eye wall hugged us tightly. At last, we knew that Katrina was going away from us.

Ever so slowly, Katrina's winds abated and about 2–3 p.m., we were able to go outside for a look around. Darrel Kinchin and I took a gas powered "workhorse" golf cart to survey the damage. With all of the twisted, fallen trees and downed power lines, we could not move more than one block from the Club in either direction. The devastation was incredible! "Oh my, this will take weeks to clean up," I thought, not yet knowing the full extent of the storm.

Gradually, people began to emerge from their homes and some with chain saws beginning to cut and clear debris from the roads. Some houses were covered with trees. The roads were covered with trees. Diamondhead, who had so many trees, was now paying the price of having a beautiful city with trees.

It was all too impossible to contemplate!

That afternoon is a blur to me. I know I managed to take a look at my house, but I do not remember going there. I do remember getting two flat tires on the drive back to the house later that Monday night.

A few Diamondhead POA workers met at the fire station and immediately put their heads together to determine what should be done first and to begin checking out the damage.

The Fire Department began clearing the roads using the heavy equipment we had dispersed before the storm. Chief Westbrook from the Fire Station asked me about boats. "Why would you need boats," I asked. "Because there are people on rooftops who need rescuing," was the answer. This did not mean anything to me at that time and I only wondered for a short second about why people would be on their rooftops. I could not relate this to mean that some areas of Diamondhead were under water.

After The Storm, Monday Afternoon, August 29

Ten firemen, stationed at the Diamondhead fire hall during the storm, waited for Katrina to play herself out so they could begin checking out the community. The occupants of the building watched as neighboring buildings were being destroyed in the horrific winds. Power poles were crashing onto streets leaving exposed wires everywhere, tangled among the downed tree limbs. The fire station building, with a new roof, was well supported to sustain the horrible winds.

Just before the eye was to hit Waveland, about 11:30 a.m., the rescue workers began to receive calls from cell phones from people trapped on rooftops. They received a report that the eye was slightly to the west of Diamondhead, which meant that this area was receiving the most amount of water. The men had to wait for the eye to pass and the wind to calm down to about 70 miles per hour before it was safe to venture out into the storm. "Now we have to go. We need to get to these people before the storm reverses and the winds become powerful again," yelled Chief Westbrook.

A backhoe and one small dump truck had been left at the station for use after the storm, but they had no boat. Three rescue workers commandeered a boat stored in the nearby parking lot; and under terrible wind conditions, they managed to get the boat, with a huge motor attached, into the dump truck.

A backhoe led the way to Banyan Street, near the Devil's Elbow area, where the first call had come from. Pushing aside debris enough to get the small truck through, they soon encountered streets flooded with water, sometimes as high as the truck bed. When they neared the small lake to the north of Banyan Street, they could not identify where the banks had been. This area had already flooded before the eye of Katrina reached Diamondhead.

About 11:30 a.m., the second crew of rescue people headed towards the south side to look for a boat. They had to turn back before they reached the interstate. Much to their surprise, they could see that water was up to the second floor air conditioning units of the Comfort Inn! They also noticed that the interstate was under water to the west; and as they looked to the east, it was the same thing, the highway was under water.

The men then headed for the northern area of Diamondhead where they thought they knew of a boat they could use. Heading through the eastern area of the city, they were flagged down by people standing outside on the street who reported people who needed medical attention.

In the first hour, they removed several truckloads of people. One house had six people in it and the other about five. The houses were flooded and some had collapsed. This team of rescuers then went to help the crew working on the westside of Diamondhead.

A boat came floating down into someone's back yard, complete with a motor that started, and was soon commandeered by this second team of firemen. Wading through water up to their waists and dodging flying debris was difficult and hazardous, and removing people hanging onto rooftops was perilous as the winds were still blowing. Many people, especially children, could not move as shock had taken over. Some of these people had been hanging on for several hours while tremendous winds attempted to blow them into the high water. Some people had partly fallen through the floor of the attic as their feet broke through the ceiling of the floor below. Many had to be rescued for medical reasons.

The rescued people were taken to a "dry house" on the corner of Analii and Diamondhead Drive North. The Presbyterian Church, also known as the Community Church, was opened and the rescued were transported in small cars and the small fire department pickup truck to the church. Soon, they were being told that this church was full; there was no more room and the Baptist Church and the Community Center were opened to serve the needy.

By early evening, the boats began to drag as the water receded to about 2 feet. Members of the Fire Department continued rescuing people and helping the injured until darkness fell and it became too dangerous to be on the streets. Some people refused to come down from attics and they had to be rescued the next morning. Some 200 people were rescued by the local fire department.

All cars that had been parked in the flooded areas before the storm were flooded and not operating. Many people walked out of this flooded area and were then taken to a church or walked the way themselves. One gentleman, who wore only a bathing suit, had held his head against the ceiling of his house with the water under his chin, thinking his next move was to swim out before he drowned, but then the water stopped rising.[2]

Monday night (the night of the storm), about 35 people slept on the floor of the Community Center in wet clothing. Chris Marz went home, grabbed all of the bedding and towels that she could find and returned to the center. That night everyone in the Baptist Church ate frozen treats from the Dairy Queen as the owner realized that he was about to lose everything with no refrigeration. When Chris and Chip left the church that night, the refugees were left with only one flashlight for light and one bucket to carry to the duck pond for water to flush the toilets.

Monday night was a hot, sticky night, making it difficult to sleep.

Timeline for Diamondhead, August 29

3:15 a.m. Tornado passes over Diamondhead

6:07 a.m. An intense rain band spawning tornadoes all along the Coast

5:30 a.m. Water coming into Salsbury garage—Southside

5:30 a.m. Power goes off

7:30 a.m. Water into homes north of Airport Drive

9:00 a.m. Water under doors on west side

10:00 a.m. Water on Kome Drive

10:15–10:30 a.m. Height of Katrina

11:00 a.m. Water at its highest in South Diamondhead

11:30 a.m. Salsbury home breaks up

11:30–12:15 a.m. Sun came out on west side for about one minute as eye passes over (Estimated time as no one was looking at their watches)

3 p.m. Water recedes from west side

6:00 p.m. Still 5 feet of water on area south of Airport Drive

Beaten by Wind and Water—Diamondhead Destruction

Most of Diamondhead was spared from the water and flooding, but only a handful of homes escaped the wind and tornadoes. Most homes had roof damage; and soon Diamondhead, like most cities on the coast, was sporting blue tarps. Most out buildings and fences were blown down or crushed by fallen trees. At least one half of the trees in Diamondhead were down or broken off at about the 20–30 feet level; many were uprooted.

Blue tarps were seen everywhere as most Diamondhead homes had some roof damage. (Photo by Fagan)

The Country Club had sections of its roof blown away, and there was water damage inside the building, leaving it unusable.

Lanai Village was heavily wind damaged with some roof sections blown away. One building caved into its first floor. Some units had water damage inside as water entered through the damaged roofs. Three weeks later, one building of eight units burned down when workers went into the building to do repair work. High Point had one building with major damage and a few had roof damage. Lakeside, Molokai and Kono Villages had very little damage.

Diamondhead south of I-10 is gone. The massive tidal wave, with a storm surge of 23–26 feet slammed into the beaches south of Diamondhead at Bay St. Louis and Waveland. The winds, at 150 miles per hour, pushed the waters of the Bay of St. Louis over its banks, into many homes of Diamondhead and left some areas looking like that of Hiroshima in 1945. Katrina left only about a dozen houses, all north of Airport Drive, partially standing; but all were heavily damaged. More than 225 homes and condominiums were lost in this area.

Most of the homes closest to the Bay of St. Louis, had been built to sustain a Category 4 hurricane, but they could not survive the horrible storm water that Katrina delivered. It did not matter if a home was built of brick or wood, splintered lumber was strewn everywhere. The wooded area to the north was littered with clothes, plastic, pieces of roofing and boats flung into the trees. There were a few toilets, some furniture and appliances to be found, but much of the contents of these 225–250 homes were distributed into the Bay of St. Louis or the Gulf of Mexico as the water receded.

For months following the storm, this area was an eerie site, especially at night, as there was no electricity or streetlights. Clothes swung in the trees in the breeze like bizarre Halloween decorations. A few residents were able to live in their upper floors. After several weeks, a few more owners began to return, setting up trailers and tents, attempting to protect what little was left of their property. Many will never return or rebuild. Some say that the trauma and memories are too great. Life is not worth the effort to evacuate or the amount of worry when another storm threatens to return to the coast. Few had enough insurance to rebuild what they once had; sadly some had no flood insurance at all.

The airport hangar was damaged, but the runway was fine and was able to be used soon after the storm. Many residents owned their own airplanes and housed them in hangars behind or beneath their homes. Only 4–5 planes were flown out before Katrina hit, and the 22 that remained were flung into the trees to the north or crushed under the debris of the hangars. Many boats and cars left on the south side suffered the same destruction.

The swimming pools and finger canals were found filled with smashed cars, washing machines, trees and other debris. Six months later, some of these have yet to be cleaned out.

All ditches around Diamondhead were found filled with strange items.
(Photo by Author)

The Yacht Club, overlooking the beautiful Bay of St. Louis, is gone; only the roof remains, still supported by pillars or the piers that the building was built on. The Marina docks and piers were destroyed along with the Ship's Store and airport hangar.

When Hurricane evacuations are ordered, the yachts docked at the Diamondhead Marina are moved to the *"hurricane hole"* on the Rotten Bayou, near the Devils Elbow area. Nineteen boats were moved before Katrina, under the direction of Capt. Stan Wormuth. They were lashed together front to back, side to side and thought to be in a safe harbor. After searching for several weeks using small boats, the boats were not to be found. It was only by satellite maps were they located, still all together, almost as they had been left, but about three quarters of a mile to the northwest on the other side of the Jourdan River. They were in the trees and not visible from the river or from any roads. When Hurricane Rita was scheduled to arrive on September 24, two boats were floated out on the high water.

It was one year after Katrina that the remaining 16 boats, one houseboat had to be demolished, were removed from this area by dredging a narrow canal to get them back on water and float them out.

The Comfort Inn south of the highway and all buildings in the shopping center were either destroyed or flooded and unusable.

The Casino Magic golf course carts had been moved onto the entertainment barge, near the Casino at Bay St. Louis. This barge was pushed by the strong winds of Katrina, across the Bay of St. Louis, and into the southeast area of Diamondhead. Trucks and small trailers were used to rescue 61 of the 73 carts. The barge is still stuck at Diamondhead.

Along Diamondhead Drive North, the area of Bayou Drive, Anela, Analii, and Mahalo Hui Drive and other streets closest to the Jourdan River, was hit extremely hard by flooding. This area was not listed as flood area, on the flood plain maps, prior to the storm. All property owners, north of I-10, thought their homes to be safe from flooding. However, Mother Nature pushed the water from the Bay into the rivers, bayous and sloughs, which could not hold any more water, spilling it into the low lands of Diamondhead. Here the water rose from three to twenty-five feet. During a hurricane, a river such as the Jourdan, reverses its flow of water. In normal weather the water flows toward the south, but when the hurricane winds of Katrina pushed the water from the Bay of St. Louis into the mouth of the Jourdan, the two flows of water met, which resulted in a much higher level of water. Nearly 8 inches of rainwater was funneled into the river from the streets of Diamondhead, creating even more water with nowhere for it to go except out of its banks, across lawns and into vulnerable homes.

While the water remained in the houses, everything, including refrigerators, mattresses, books, etc., was floating around the rooms. When the water receded, it left everything in the home soaked, strewn around in a layer of mud and in a hodge-podge array. Many times, large items, such as refrigerators, were found to be blocking doorways, making it impossible to get into those rooms.

The water left within a few hours; but without electricity the extreme heat and humidity soon caused mold to appear on everything. Dead animals, such as wild pigs, deer, family pets and armadillos had been washed into yards, and a stench, unmentionable, began to settle over these areas. Clothes swung in trees as if they had been hung there to dry.

Kome Drive homes were not spared, as 4–16 feet of water from the Jourdan River area was forced into these homes, rising to the top of some second story structures. All homes on this street were flooded by water backing up from the same drainage ditches designed to keep these homes dry, but they ultimately turned into pathways for Katrina's rush of water. Those who stayed through the storm on this street were forced to swim to higher ground.

The area on Diamondhead Drive East, from Molakai Village to the tennis courts, was heavily damaged when the Bay waters flowed across I-10 and into their yards and homes. Five homes were completely smashed when their roofs collapsed into the lower floors. Fifty homes were flooded or destroyed in this area.

Diamondhead had a total of 465 homes flooded or water driven into them on the north side of Hwy 10 and about 230 homes south of the Highway.

The Oaks received a lot of water from the Rotten Bayou leaving many homes unlivable. Those along Noma Drive were flooded with 2–8 feet of water. Some people had to swim out of these homes to reach high ground.

The Diamondhead Mall, or main business district of Diamondhead, was badly damaged by the wind. Most buildings had walls blown out or roofs off. The Aloha Gallery lucked out with only the outside sign blown away. Inside the gallery a stone building block fell from the wall and landed in a jewelry case, miraculously doing no damage.

Residents with boats from the south side had moved them to the Diamondhead Shopping Center parking lot prior to the storm. About 100 boats were parked there. After Katrina, these boats were helter-skelter and upside down, scattered everywhere.

The Ramada Inn was heavily damaged, but about 200 people managed to ride out the storm in the building. The Burger King area was not flooded, but many buildings in this area were damaged by high winds.

Tennis World received 28 feet of water, which washed over the roof of the tennis structure, destroying the building. The tennis courts fared well and were soon being used. Efforts are being looked into to rebuild Tennis World closer to the Country Club area.

Many of the street and traffic signs throughout Diamondhead were gone; roads were damaged and streetlights missing or damaged. Some areas look as though a tornado touched down at that point and probably did.

The golf courses were heavily damaged with hundreds of downed trees. The Pine course opened about the middle of October and the Cardinal front nine opened in December, followed by the back nine the following February.

Trees—trees and more downed trees. They were everywhere, especially across the roads, making them impassible. Most grass and shrubs had turned brown from the salt water. Diamondhead lost thousands of trees, mostly pine, which had been twisted and snapped halfway up the trunk line. However, the stately oak tree fared quite well. Mother Nature must have known what she was doing when she designed these trees to flex in the wind. Most oaks were left standing but with branches broken away. They were all denuded of their leaves and stripped of the Spanish moss that had clung to their branches.

Wrapping their arms around a tree, one resident and his son, rode out the storm in the raging water on the south side of Diamondhead while attempting to keep their heads above water. The debris was constantly slamming into their backs. They survived!

Gene and Leona Wolfe, ages 70 and 67, decided to stay and ride out the storm in their home on Airport Road south of I10 in Diamondhead. They had lived in their home for 15 years and never had any water even near their house during previous heavy rains. They had weathered many hurricanes while living in New Orleans. Despite the warnings being issued all weekend, they felt very secure about staying for Katrina. Their wood frame house was built on three-foot cinder blocks and the garage on a slab, both 12 feet above sea level

Gene's airplane was resting in his hangar behind the house, ready to take off for his next flight. Gene felt that he had prepared for the worst. Leona was not so sure. She wanted to leave.

Gene's sister had been visiting the home the week before the

Thousands of pine trees were broken off 20–30 feet in air.
(Photo by author)

storm. About 4 p.m. Saturday afternoon her daughter arrived to take her to a safer place.

When Saturday night approached and the winds were picking up, Gene moved several mattresses, sofa cushions and an ax into a central hallway. He gathered up a small portable radio along with other necessary items to use if the electricity failed.

Gene and Leona settled down for the night. The radio was giving them up to date news of the storm, and about 2:30 a.m. a tornado was reported about to hit the Diamondhead area. About 5:30 a.m. the power went off. Checking on the house, Gene discovered water, about two feet deep, in the garage. The two cars in the garage began to float into each other and bang around, and the headlights came on. He could hear the fan motor running in one of the cars, which gave off a burning odor.

About 7:30 a.m., water was coming through the floor of the house, buckling the wood floors, which were popping and going poof, poof. They decided to go into the attic that was above the bedroom and bath areas. The trim was being torn off from above the windows by the wind. At this time, they heard a terrible noise near the rear of the house; it could have been a tree blown onto the roof.

The water was moving up the front yard, not sitting water like a lake, but advancing along the ground. As the water quickly rose, Gene noticed that there was no water on the deck. He realized later that the deck was probably floating at this time, staying above the water line.

The two began to panic and they began to run around picking up things from the floor and placing them on top of tall furniture. Leona grabbed a small purse and filled it with precious papers, such as driver's license, credit cards and what cash they had in the house, forgetting about her rings in a drawer. They made their way to the attic.

The attic was practically empty except for one box of extension cords used for previous Christmas lights, a set of metal crutches and 2 queen size foam mattress pads, each about 3 inches thick.

Gene soon discovered that he had forgotten the ax and went back down stairs to find it. It was not where he had left it and he began to panic. In knee-deep water, he ran into the kitchen to find anything that he could use to chop a hole in the roof. After desperately searching through all drawers, the only thing he could find was a meat cleaver with a bone saw attached and a butcher knife.

Back in the attic, Gene desperately began to search the roof for a place to break through and chose a spot on the east end of the building. (Later he discovered this to be a very wise choice) He attempted to open a section of roof by pushing the knife through cracks between the panels to make some opening. With no luck, he desperately grabbed one of the crutches, and after about 30 minutes of beating on one panel, he managed to get a small section to lift up about 6 inches. He was able to hold it there. During this time, he told his wife to unroll the mattress pads, roll each up tightly like a rolled newspaper and tie one tightly around each of their waists.

Then a gust of wind got under the edge of the panel that Gene was holding open and ripped away the entire 4 x 8 foot panel of roofing, tumbling it over and over into the sky toward the east, over his neighbor's home. This created a large opening in the roof, and it soon began to come apart and fly away.

The siding of the house was coming off, and Gene noticed the attic stairs were floating up and banging against the top of the ceiling. They could hear the furniture from downstairs bumping against the ceiling and the floor of the attic. Soon the rest of the east side of the roof pealed off and blew over the top of them. Luckily, they were on the right side of the attic, as they would have been crushed if they had been on the west side of the eave.

"The roof was shaking like crazy," said Leona "and the house was shifting from its supports."

At this point, it looked like they were going to drown. They could see the water lapping against the eaves outside the house. They knew that they would have to get out of what was left of this house, somehow. They jumped into the very cold and dirty water with the mattresses tied around their waists.

The next thing Gene remembers is holding onto a piece of roofing, being propelled backwards by the wind, held up by the water and the mattresses tied around their waists. Debris was spinning through the air. Pieces of houses, doors and furniture were flying around them. They were being swept by the fast current across three empty lots to the west of their house, covered with tall trees prior to Katrina. They saw no trees as they were propelled along as they were above the trees that were left standing. They had all they could do to keep their heads above the water with the wind howling and screaming around them.

Somehow, the wind and waves had kept them together; and all at once, they came to an abrupt halt! The water was tearing around them, but they were held still. Leona began to scream that she was hurting and Gene discovered that the submerged mattress, tied around her waist, was caught on a busted-off pine tree. She was being strangled as it was being pulled tighter and tighter by the force of strong water.

Leona was being held horizontally by the caught mattress and pushed backwards by the water, causing her head to go under the water. Gene began holding her head up to keep her from drowning. Leona said at this point, "We are going to drown; I can't make it." "Then we will drown together," screamed Gene over the sound of the wind. There was a branch hanging over them from another tree and Gene told Leona to hold onto that branch. The water was rocking them back and forth.

The brackish water was covered with a huge amount of marsh grass, which kept building up around their faces and threatening to shut off their breathing. Gene kept pulling this marsh grass out of Leona's nose and mouth and also from around his face as the grass threatened to cover their heads.

Leona kept screaming, "This cord is cutting me so bad, you have to cut it off." Gene tried to untie the wet knots in her cord, but found this to be impossible.

Gene, dressed only in a pair of pants and no shirt, braced himself against the tree that they were caught on and he began to tear away at her foam mattress with his finger nails, piece by little piece, while trying to keep their heads above water and clearing the marsh grass away from their faces. The current and waves of the water were very strong, slamming him continually against the rough bark of the tree.

About this time something caught the band of his watch on his left arm and threatened to break his hold from the tree. When the band did not break under this pressure, he let go with his right hand to reach over and slip off his watch before he was taken away in the current.

He began to have some success with breaking away the foam on the mattress and was soon able to release her from the terrible pressure and she could then breathe freely. It was not until later that Gene realized that he had a pocketknife in his pocket all this time and could have cut her loose earlier, but he had forgotten about it.

They continued to hold onto pieces of roofing as they watched other homes around them break up and blow away. After one hour and 45 minutes of being in the water, the wind began to calm down, but they were then totally disoriented. Even though it was daylight and they could see well enough, they had no bearings as to where they were. Everything looked strange.

***

"Oh God, your sea is so great and my boat is so small!" (Unknown)

***

They knew they had been blown to the west and decided to try to edge their way eastward. They began to climb over debris in about 25 feet of water. Slipping off pieces of debris, they would grab onto anything that they could reach.

They soon became tired, completely out of breath, and decided to rest. They climbed onto a platform created by two trees nesting together, pulled a large board over to rest their feet upon, and were as comfortable as could be.

The weather began to change and the air turned to freezing. It was a bone-chilling cold, something that does not occur in August on the Coast. Neither of them had any shoes on. Gene had no shirt, only pants, she only a thin gown. Their teeth began to chatter as the wind continued to whistle around them. Gene grabbed several wet pieces of insulation and wrapped it around their shoulders to help keep the wind off.

Meanwhile their neighbor, Paul Russell, had also decided to not evacuate. He boarded up his home, on Sunday, for the third time during the summer. The previous two storms had been all hype and no fury, and he felt that he would be fine staying in his home for this storm. His house was 14 feet above sea level with the main living quarters on the second floor, which should be high enough to keep out any water. He convinced his son, Steve, who had come down from Jackson to help board up the house, to stay with him.

Before he came to Diamondhead, Steve had loaded up two generators, which were still in the bed of his truck sitting in the driveway. Cable service went out on Sunday evening, but they were getting a local channel using rabbit ears. An uncle in Indiana was keeping in constant touch with them by cell phone, updating them on the storm, location, etc.

About 5:30 a.m. on Monday morning, the power went off and Steve cranked up a generator to keep a fan going as it was so hot. A neighbor, Lynn Nelson, came over for a cup of coffee and they convinced her to stay at their home for the rest of the storm. She had left with nothing, just the clothes on her back, as she thought she was going to return to her home. After one cup of coffee, Lynn decided to go home and noticed that the water was up to the fourth step and she could not get home. The generator quit and all was quiet except for the howling wind, which seemed to "suck the air right out of your lungs," described Steve.

The three calmly watched the storm. There was very little panic and the thought that the house might break up never occurred to any of them. There were even a few humorous moments, but then one of the sliding glass door panels blew in and the house was exposed to the elements. The water kept rising, as if it were coming out of the ground. There was no 30-foot high water surge; it just kept rising and rising fast!

And the winds were fierce!

Steve later said, "No words can possibly describe what it was like during the storm. Even the smell was indescribable."

They received a call from Steve's uncle, who told them that the eye would be passing over them in a few minutes and they should expect a calm period in the weather. When this happened, the sun almost came out. The water was at its peak height and filled with swells. They watched as Lynn's house next door imploded and caved in.

Then the group noticed that the Wolfe house to the south and across the taxiway was gone. They knew that Gene and Leona Wolfe had stayed in their home for the storm. "Where were they?" everyone wondered. The hangar belonging to the Wolfes had caved down into itself and looked as if it had been made for little people. They began to worry about other people in the neighborhood, but they could not decide how to begin searching for them or what to do at this point. They watched a large angry pine tree slice through the house of Bob and Brenda Sell. The tree went completely through the house, down to the foundation, just as if there was nothing to stop it until it reached the ground. Bricks from the house were flying everywhere.

The three people were now holding down the furniture, which was floating in three feet of water on the second floor. The stove was floating; shoes were coming out of the closets; carpet was floating and everything was threatening to wash out of the open door as the wind began to reverse and take everything with it as it left for the coast.

Using binoculars, Steve noticed someone standing up in a tree. This man, with no shirt on, stood out like a beacon among the debris. They soon determined that it was Gene Wolfe.

"We have to get him," related Steve. The thought that they would be better off where they were did not occur to them. "No, we have to, somehow, rescue Gene and his wife." They packed some clothes, placed them into a garbage bag with a twist tie and attached it to Steve's belt and he jumped into the water.

At this point, the water was reversing and was retreating down the taxiway, extremely fast, toward the Bay of St. Louis. Under these conditions, Steve could only make it to the taxiway and headed back to the house. The bag of clothes had torn from his waist.

He bumped into something slippery and smooth in the water. (He was thinking it was something else.) It was Lynn's car, which had broken windows, and he badly cut his hand. Returning to the house, they refilled another bag, this time a Wal-Mart bag, and once again he jumped into the swirling water, swimming from tree to tree, but making no headway to the west and south where the Wolfes had been seen.

He then allowed the current to take him towards the east, past Lynn's house, where he could now make his way across the taxiway and then he was able to make his way towards the west and the stranded couple.

Ducking under a downed tree, he bobbed up in the water, and could see the freezing couple with few clothes on. "Hey," he yelled and

Gene Wolfe painfully relating his horrible experience delivered by Katrina (Photo by Baur)

plopped the bag of clothes onto the platform formed by the downed trees.

"Did you bring lunch?" asked Gene.

Gene's version:

After about 10 to 15 minutes, Gene decided to stand up on the trees they were stranded on, and try to get his bearings. Looking around he saw a house across the rushing river of water to the north. There were three people standing on the second floor of a partial balcony. They were looking at the river below, on what was previously the airplane taxi run, flowing fiercely past them. One of the three saw Gene and began to wave.

Gene waved back to them, raising two fingers to indicate that there were two people on the tree.

Gene sat back down, attempting to keep warm, not knowing what to do and wondering how they would ever get out of this situation. After about 20 minutes he was amazed to see, about 25 feet away, a young man's head pop up in the water. It was Steve Russell swimming towards them from the house Gene had spotted a few minutes earlier.

"We need to get you to our house," said Steve. Gene replied, "How can we do this? My wife will never make it." "Well, we will do it somehow," said Steve.

The three rested for a time, pondering what to do. Birds began arriving, flying around them and landing on the trees. They noticed many ice chests floating in the water and Gene snagged a large chest. He told his wife to hang onto one handle and he would hang onto the other handle, while hanging onto Steve, who would lead the way across, what was the airplane taxi run, but now an open river of water. There was little debris in the water between the two houses. The water was beginning to recede and the wind was reversing direction. The water was only about eight feet deep and much easier to swim in. "Kick like hell," said Steve "and hang on." They found they could bob down, touch the ground, bounce back up and proceed this way across the taxiway.

Badly scratched and bleeding, they made their way to the broken and wobbly steps under the battered Russell home. Exhausted and hurting they climbed up and joined Paul Russell and Lynn Nelson. The second floor of the house had three feet of water in it during the height of the storm. Within three to four hours, the water was gone leaving only a wet taxiway below them. However, the water had left about 5 inches of mud on the floor.

Al Roche, who lived just to the east, had also stayed for the storm and survived in the attic of his house, which was not completely destroyed. He was badly cut up, with one bad cut on his arm, but basically fine. He joined the group, which made a total of six people. They lived in the house for the next three days.

No one came to get them. The debris outside was too difficult to climb over as it was 20 feet high with jagged, dangerous edges with nails sticking out of everything. Gene and Leona were badly beaten and unable to walk more than a few yards. Gene had been badly cut across his back as he was wedged against the tree that they were tied to for so long a period. This tree did save them from being taken farther into danger. He also had one long scratch, probably from a nail, on his right foot.

For three days, they stared out onto the devastation, through the empty hole in the wall where the windows had been, not believing what they saw before them and in total shock. They felt as thought they were in a stupor and did not know what to do. There was enough food in the refrigerators and they had bottled water. Paul had just obtained 200 pounds of fresh shrimp for an outing for the next weekend. The shrimp was available along with other food in the freezers. Some, though, did not feel like eating.

Helicopters were spotted flying over the area, and the men tried unsuccessfully to signal them.

They were sleeping on wet mattresses, could not brush their teeth and had only one bucket of water, which was muddy, to wash their hands. Gene and Leona were covered with a black sludge that was impossible to wash off and took days to scrape off. This mud stayed in their hair until they were able to take showers days later. They made several trips to a ditch behind the house for water to flush the toilets, but by Thursday, that water was beginning to dry up.[3]

JoAnn and Tony Vaz, and their dog, Fergie, lived nearby, on Akoko St., in a ground level brick home. They had been watching the storm since daybreak from their large front porch. The wind, which had come up during the night, had a horrible scream and was terrible to hear. It was driving the rain in sheets, parallel to the ground. They watched all of the pine trees across the street fall over across the power lines. Like dominos, they fell one by one.

The Vaz' decided that they needed to leave the house. They began to grab items such as medicines, her handbag, along with a hamper of clothes and some towels. Tony loaded a generator and a can of gas into the back of his pickup. The water was beginning to creep up the lawn, a little at a time, and by the time the truck was loaded with the few items, the water was up to the top of the tires. As they left, the roof of their house, felt like it was being torn away.

They could not drive down the street as they usually did because of the downed trees, and the sky looked like as if a tornado was approaching. They decided to move to the Jean Durr home. With her windows boarded up, Jean had evacuated the day before and had always told the Vaz' that they could take refuge in her home if they ever found the need.

They carried up the generator and hamper of clothes. The water was thigh high and filled with many small animals looking for safety. The main living quarters on the second floor of the house seemed to be high enough to keep out any amount of water. Immediately, they noticed that the house was leaking. The second story was built with wall-to-wall windows and the wind was blowing the panes away from the frames, causing the glass to bow. Water was streaming down the windows and walls even though the windows had all been boarded up on the outside.

The house was shaking, and the ceiling fans were swinging crazily back and forth. They began to move small items to the third floor, where the master bedroom was located. They then sat on the stair-well and watched their 32-foot sailboat, that had been stored in Jean's hangar, float away in the water. The lights came on in their truck and then slowly went out again. The burglar alarm on the house began to go off. It blared and blared, but they could barely here it above the screeching wind.

In addition, the incredible wind continued to scream and blow. They watched Jean's beautiful antiques dancing in the water. Suddenly they heard the glass break on the patio doors, which wrapped all across the front of the house. The outside boards quickly blew away. (The glass broke before the boards blew away)

Once the glass broke, the house stopped shaking, but the water was still there. The house became open to the elements, and items that were floating around in the rooms began to float out the open spaces. The refrigerator floated down the stair well and wedged there. The back deck floated away. The water was one-half way up the second floor of the house before it began to recede.

About 3:30 p.m., they were able to walk out of the house and stand in the mud. The water was gone, completely. As they walked to where their home should have been, everywhere they looked; there were huge piles of debris. Their home was gone, completely gone, as were their neighbors' homes. A 40 x 20 foot greenhouse filled with orchids was gone, nothing left.

Gone with the wind, or, was it the water?

Even though the homes on Akoko were higher in elevation than those to the west, all the homes along Akoko were gone, while some to the west were there, but barely standing.

Tony had been building an airplane in their hangar. They did find JoAnn's black funeral dress, still in the plastic bag, still on its hanger, flying in a tree. It was not even damp or muddy. An afghan, made by Tony's mother was lying on a tree, as if it had been spread there to air.

On Tuesday morning, they discovered Lynn Nelson's dog near a debris pile. Lynn had given up hope of ever seeing it again.

Tony and JoAnn remained in Jean's house until Thursday when

What is left of home, yard and greenhouse of Tony and JoAnn Vaz
(Photo by Izydorek)

they left the area. About the second day after the storm, Gene Wolfe and Lynn Nelson made a trip over the debris piles to the Durr home, where the Vaz' were staying. They borrowed some dry clothes, water, etc. and a garden wagon in the debris, loaded the items up and pulled this cart along with them over the piles of debris to return to the Russell home. The Vaz's later moved to Lucedale where they may relocate. They definitely will not rebuild on the south side. JoAnn says that her plants will not grow there any more because of the salt water. Katrina killed everything she had planted and grown for the past 19 years.

JoAnn returned several times during the following months to work in the yard, but as she would work, the memories would get to her. She would cry a little and pray a little. One day she heard a "mew" in the grass. It was a stray cat she had taken in before the storm. Once again, it needed a home.[4]

The Wolfe home was completely gone; all of it had been blown away or washed into the woods to the west. They later found a set of china, with only one piece missing. Gene's grand player piano was found in the woods to the west. Their hangar, which was behind their house to the north, had collapsed, and Gene's airplane had been washed down the taxiway, to the runway on the west side of this area and ended upside down in a ditch.

The Wolfe airplane, or what was left of it. (Photo by Wolfe)

Another couple from the south side who stayed during the storm was Dennis and Mimi Pedersen, along with their 21-year-old son, Shawn. They survived in the upstairs of their house. During the height of the storm, they debated about what to do. They tied themselves together with rope in the event that they would have to swim out. Mimi could not swim; she was terrified and believed that they were all going to drown.

The day after the storm Dennis and Shawn made their way to the north side of Diamondhead, came back with a tractor-front-end loader and began pushing debris to the side of the streets to make a small path to reach their home. They then moved to a second home of theirs on the north side of Diamondhead. They returned on Wednesday, in a small car, taking the Wolfe and Russell group to bathe in the community swimming pool. There they met other people who were washing clothes in the pool. When someone tried to make everyone leave the pool, explaining that the water was unsanitary, the thought was, *we have no water where we came from and what we had was much dirtier than this, and this feels so good. No way are we leaving.* At this time, they did not know that many other refugees, such as themselves, were staying in the Baptist Church and meals were being served there. No one related this information to them and they felt as though they had nowhere else to go except back to the wet, dirty, beaten up home of the Russells.[5]

On Thursday Elise Breen, knowing that these people were still on the south side, came looking for them. Elise was able to drive only so far, then walked the rest of the way over and around debris and eventually found the group. They told her that they needed cars to evacuate to the home of relatives. Elise had a full tank of gas and offered to drive Gene and Tony as far as needed.

The three drove to Lafayette before they found a rental agency. The gas tank on Elise's car was on empty and they were getting worried.

The dealership would not let Gene have a car as he could not prove that he had insurance on his own car. Tony was able to get a van. They loaded this van with over $650 worth of food, clothes and medicines and headed back to Diamondhead, arriving there at 11:30 that night.

Stopped at the south entrance to Diamondhead by the Alabama State Police, they were not allowed to enter. Frustrated, tired and worried, they argued that people were waiting for them to bring in the supplies stored in the back of the van. A Sergeant was called, but he would not even get out of his car. They showed their drivers licenses, which gave their street addresses, but to no avail. He laughed at them, saying, "We have been back there. There is no one there. Anyone back there is dead." He threatened to arrest them if they did not leave.

They then decided that they were not going to be able to enter through the regular entrance to the south side and left. They parked on Interstate 10 near the airport runway and agreed to walk in from the west. Here they found two feet of mud that they could have made it through, but decided against leaving the car with all of the purchases. They fell asleep in the car, along with thousands of mosquitoes and woke very early on Friday morning. Once again, the same men from the Alabama State Police were on duty and refused to let them into the area of their homes.

They tried the Property Owners Association (POA) office building with no luck. It was suggested that they try the fire department. There they found Mike Munger on duty. Gene explained to Mike their plight, and their need to get supplies into the south side area, one being his wife, etc. Mike said, "There are no people on the south side; we made the rounds back there and there are no survivors in that area. "Well, you just get me through that police line and I will prove to you that there are people still back there," said Gene.

"O.K. lets go," said Mike. Jumping on a four-wheeler, he led them through the police line, where the Sergeant very reluctantly let them pass. The only way to get to the Russell house was to go all the way to the airport circle, zig zagging around debris piles, then north on the runway, turn east on a taxi way and continue around more debris piles until the house was spotted. Mike was led up the wobbly stairs and into the house where he met Paul, Steve, Al and Lynn who were still there. No one could have imagined that anyone was living in this area. Mike could not believe his eyes, "You have been here all of this time? We have to get you out of here."

That same day, Gene and Leona's son arrived in Diamondhead to search for his parents. At first, the Police was not going to let him in either. After much arguing and threatening to swim through the swamp from the west, he was allowed to go in. As he approached the lot where the house previously sat, he was shocked to see the house was gone. He knew his parents were in that home during the storm. He noticed that all three cars were there, though in bad condition, and he began to sift through debris. He found his mother's wedding ring.

Hearing a noise to the north, he walked back and found it was coming from the house of the Russells. There he found his mother; his father had left with Tony to attempt to find a car to rent. He learned that his parents had been staying there for the past three days. He left to get some fresh water and ice for the group and then returned to take his mother to his home in Lacombe, Louisiana.

After the storm Leona's brother Jim, was plagued by Gene's sister, Mitzie, to go to Diamondhead and search for Gene and Leona. Mitzie knew they were there as she had left them along with her daughter, Bonnie, only hours before Katrina hit the coast. Jim finally agreed to travel from Mandeville to Diamondhead on Friday. When he arrived, security would not let him in; but by then, they had heard that the Wolfes were alive and had left the area.

Bonnie had put their photos and names on the internet as lost victims of Katrina and had started a club in Pensacola and named it "Little St. Bernard's Parish." She and others raised funds, collected needed items and made several trips to Diamondhead leaving the items at the Baptist Church.

Al Roche was picked up by someone in Louisiana; Lynn Nelson's cousin flew in to pick her up. It was lately determined that a total of 15 people had stayed during the storm in their homes on the south side, or at least until the water drove them out of them. Moreover, they all survived![6]

Survival During the First Week

After most storms, the clouds break up and the most beautiful weather shines down on the scene of devastation. So it was at Diamondhead on Tuesday morning.

Most of the birds appeared to be gone, and the squirrels had disappeared. It was weeks before they gradually began to return. However, the geese and ducks were around shortly after the storm, conducting business as usual, greeting all who came through the entrance of Diamondhead. That was the first glimmer of light to be seen by those who had remained behind.

What was once a "green" city had become a "brown" city. The salt water had turned everything to brown.

Those residents who tried to get back into Diamondhead had to use chain saws to make pathways through the streets. Trucks could move only a few feet at a time, as trees were cut into small portions and moved manually to allow one lane of traffic to advance. Many began to use golf carts to get around, driving them through yards and around trees. This measure also conserved gas, which was extremely scarce.

The area along Kapalama Drive was a canopy of trees. The lower branches were cut off to allow cars and trucks to pass under pine trees and utility wires.

Thousands of transformers and utility poles were toppled and destroyed. More than a million people in five states were without power, many for months.

There were no phones. There was no way to communicate with police or city directors. It soon became apparent, and even more so by

Typical scene of total desolation seen all along the coast.
(Photo by Condon)

the end of the week, how unprepared everyone was for this type of situation. The first few days were overbearing, and no one knew the best way to deal with anything. It was mainly—guess and go.

The desperate needs of staying alive had to be taken care of first.

Chip Marz, General Manager, reported on Tuesday, August 30:

Tuesday morning my staff began arriving at the POA offices. It was so gratifying to see some of them come into work that morning when they should have been home with their own families; I was so relieved.

I went to the Fire Station and found Chief Dennis Westbrook and Mike Collard, General Manager of the Water & Sewer District. It was hard to decide what was the most important and what should be tackled first and shock kept everyone from functioning to his or her best ability. We scheduled a noon meeting with other key community leaders to discuss what needs we had and what resources we had available to us. Meanwhile, Mark Boyd and his Facility Maintenance employees, Firemen, and Water & Sewer employees continued clearing the streets of fallen trees and other debris using POA heavy equipment. Diamondhead was lucky as its heavy equipment had not been harmed and was now usable.

At the noon meeting, we had Chief Westbrook, Mike Collard from water and sewer, Hancock County Sheriff Deputy Al Hermann, Hancock Bank VP Paul Guichet, Skip Alphonso, and POA staff of Security Capt. Reggie Fayard, Facilities Supt. Mark Boyd, Architectural & Engineering Supervisor Darrell Kinchen, and Club Manager Jeff Hall. We determined that the major focus would be to continue to clear the roads. This would facilitate ongoing rescue operations by the Fire Dept. It would also enable both electric companies and our Water & Sewer Department to reach their equipment and restore service expeditiously. Al Hermann and Reggie Fayard took on the law enforcement and security responsibilities, Skip Alphonso took charge of communications, and Paul Guichet helped coordinate the National Guard's food, water and ice distribution in addition to getting the bank open.

It was decided that the Fire Station would now become the Command Post, as here they had generators to keep the air conditioning going and some communication with the outside world.

What did the POA have for fuel? The fire department had some, water and sewer department had some, but all was a very short supply for what would be needed. We realized that it was very important to get electricity to the gas stations.

This group continued to meet once or twice a day over the next two weeks to set priorities, which seemed to change almost hourly!

The Electric Company arrived immediately, ready to string wires, if they could get to them. It was decided that the first places that should receive power would be the following:

1. Fire Department, functioning as Command Post of Diamondhead
2. Water & Sewer sites so that the water tower could be filled and return service
3. Gas stations, for obvious reasons
4. POA offices
5. Baptist Church relief center
6. Hancock Bank, since money was needed

Tuesday morning, it was still unclear to Marz, as to why people were coming from the northwest part of Diamondhead, some walking, some brought on truck beds, all looking for a place to stay. He later learned that many Diamondhead homes had been under high water and these people had no homes or personal items.

The fire department was still rescuing people out of attics, mostly elderly people. Attics in Diamondhead have pull down steps, and very poor floorboards once you get up there. Many could not get back down from the attic once they had used all of their efforts to get up there.

A truck with its bed filled with people drove by the Community Center, and one woman yelled, "I was just rescued off my roof." Some residents had been on their roofs for 24 hours. The firemen were still combing the streets looking for people who needed help.

The firemen also continued to clear streets as many people needed help but were trapped in cul-de-sacs by downed trees. Many needed medicine. The firemen would load up their vehicles with water, ice and food and attempt to reach the isolated areas where help was needed. The department managed to acquire some 4-wheelers, which turned out to be very useful that week.

The men began going door to door in the worst damaged areas searching for survivors. If no one was found in the home, or what was left of it, a large "C" was painted on the front door to indicate it had been searched. This continued all of Tuesday and some of Wednesday.

Early on Tuesday morning people began to show up at the door of the local drug store. Many people had left without their medications as they fled the storm. The pharmacy building had heavy roof damage. A huge industrial generator was obtained and the drug store opened on Thursday. People were standing in line to enter the store. It was reported that there were also drug addicts waiting in line looking for their fix.

A tanker from the airport, containing 10,000 gallons of fuel had been ripped from the main hangar and floated, first to the west and then up to Hwy 10, blocking several lanes of the highway. Ninety-five percent of state roads in Mississippi were impassible. However, U.S. Hwy 49 from Hattiesburg to the coast was passable for emergency vehicles the day of the storm. All other routes were open, at least with one lane, by Wednesday.

People were told not to attempt to use the roads as they were reserved for emergency vehicles and power trucks coming in from other states. However, some residents did manage to get through these checkpoints. A few people drove down from northern states a day or so after the storm, worried about the damage to their homes. They could not get near their homes, especially if they were located on the south side of the highway. These people then became a burden for everyone because there was little food and water, no electricity and no gas for them to leave the area.

The Command Center at the local fire department building was inundated with people wanting to know how the POA was handling this and/or what were they doing about that. The wife of Chief Westbrook remained by his side during the first week, writing down decisions as they were being decided on at desperate moments. Those that were not there at the moment of decision-making would be instructed from her notes as to how things were to be handled. No one else was going to challenge the chief and his committee once those decisions were decided upon. Tempers rose at times, but someone had to be on top of it. The Chief had to be gone much of the time to attend to business and others had to know the procedures to follow. It was ten days before Chief Westbrook and his wife were able to leave the Center. They had six trees on top of their house. For many Diamondhead volunteers, the suffering of the community came first.

Few people had gas to drive to a store that might have supplies and neighbors began sharing with each other. At first, there was no water, but there was food; and people were soon throwing steaks onto their grills from their freezers, before the meat spoiled. It became evident that the electricity would not be on for weeks. Many people who had evacuated had left their house keys with neighbors, etc. who began to raid these freezers knowing that the homeowners would not mind someone using the contents.

Everyone ate very well the first few days!

Diamondhead became a "safe place," a refugee center for those from the surrounding areas such as Pass Christian, Waveland and all of Hancock County. Those who were housed in the Community Center and Episcopal Church were sent to the Baptist Church, which became the Refugee Center. Anyone could go to the Baptist Church to find out about relatives or friends. There you could check the list of missing people or add someone to the list.

The Ramada Inn, roofless on the south side, still housed 200–300 people and was way over filled with people sleeping all over the building. At the height of the storm it was estimated that about 200 people took refuge here.

It was soon evident that Diamondhead was much unprepared to take in refugees. No one had ever considered that such a situation could occur.

Tents began to go up, especially near the Baptist Church, as this was where food was served. It was warm enough to sleep outside; and, for many, it would be their only shelter for a long time.

On Tuesday evening the fire department crew was called to the Jourdan River on Interstate 10 because of a car in the river. It turned out to be an 18-year-old girl from Florida, traveling east from Texas on I-10, who had flipped her car over the bridge barrier and into the river.

A state trooper happened along, stopped to check on his tire and heard someone calling for help. It was dark and very hard to see anything. She was found standing on the top of her car, with water over her feet. The car was completely underwater and had been there for about an hour. The bridge had not been damaged or marked in any way at the point where she entered the water.

The fire department took her back to the fire station, where she stayed for 3–4 days before being able to leave. Six months later the vehicle is still there.[7]

On Wednesday Fire Chief Westbrook traveled to Waveland to beg for supplies. Westbrook was the only person in Diamondhead authorized to request help from the Emergency Distribution Center that had been set up in Waveland. "There were truckloads of supplies just sitting there," said Westbrook. "We need supplies in Diamondhead," he related. One individual made the comment that all the Chief was thinking of was Diamondhead, implying that conditions were much worse in Waveland, which they were. Chief replied, "No, that is a ridiculous statement, as we not only have our refugees, but hundreds of your refugees, from all over Hancock County, who have fled to Diamondhead, for help. We have no provisions for these refugees. We do not have food, water, ice or baby formula for these people. You are forgetting about us; we need help and we need it now."

The trip had taken much time out of Chief Westbrook's day, when he was badly needed back at Diamondhead. At this time he also requested help with law enforcement for Diamondhead, as the security could not handle the problem of unruly people. He explained that Diamondhead's law enforcement people, along with the firemen, were physically worn out.

After returning to Diamondhead, Westbrook arranged for a truck to go back to Waveland and load up ice, which was then distributed at the local B.P. station. Those supplies were gone in two minutes. People came out of nowhere. No one could ever figure out how anyone knew that ice was available. The truck made several trips before an 18-wheeler arrived in Diamondhead with ice, water and food.

Donny Martin, Manager of the Supermarket, was a great help to everyone following the storm. When baby supplies were needed at the Baptist Church, Donny told them, "Just back your truck up to the back door and you can load up anything you need." Because the roof of the store had been partially blown away, a lot of water had entered the building; the volunteers were walking in 6 inches of water in a completely dark building. Supplies were used from the store for many purposes. Food that would otherwise have spoiled was given to the Baptist Church. Martin tried to keep this a secret, but he is one of the unsung heroes that helped feed so many in a time of need.

For the first week, Donny, fearing looters or people breaking into the building for cigarettes, sat on a lawn chair in front of the store, holding a hammer. By Thursday, his face was very sun burned and he needed a break. Chris Marz offered to take his place for a few minutes. Six young men drove up in a car, demanding cigarettes. They were rough, dirty looking and not people to argue with. Just as she panicked and wondered what she was going to do next, a sheriff's deputy happened to drive up, got out of his car and asked the young men if he could help them. They were gone in a second.

On Wednesday afternoon, Mark Carpenter, from Gladewater, Texas, asked to meet with the manager of Diamondhead. He had seen Chip's interview on TV the day before, telling the public that this area badly needed supplies. Mark returned to Texas, loaded a semi-trailer with water, gasoline, generators, tarps and food and delivered it to Diamondhead on Thursday. He made several trips back and forth from Texas with supplies during the next few days.

Hungry for information, people in shelters throughout the South, lined up for free newspapers. This was the only way to discover that New Orleans was not the only city that Katrina devastated. Everyone knew someone in neighboring towns and hungered for information on how bad the situation was in those areas. Papers were also the only way to find out how to obtain help. *The Sun Herald* was delivering free newspapers to the shelters.

Within a day or two it was clear that gasoline and diesel fuel were becoming scarce commodities. Both Golf Course Maintenance and all POA facilities had large tanks of each available, and they had topped them off as standard operating procedure before an approaching storm. However, those supplies were rapidly being depleted with all of the activity.

There was no gasoline at either of the two gas stations as there was no electricity to pump the gas, and there was very little gas to begin with. Everyone became gas scroungers!

Gas was in such high demand that people were siphoning gas from anything that looked as though it had a gas tank, such as deserted boats. When owners came back to retrieve their boats, they probably found the gas tanks empty. (Many residents remained during the storm primarily to protect their property from humans and Mother Nature.)

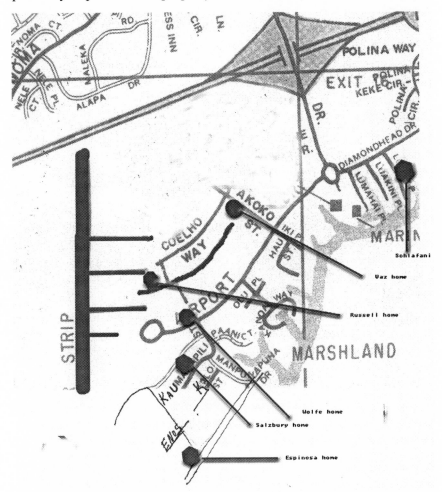

Mario and Rose Espinosa had lived in their home on Poki Place, which is right on the north edge of the Bay of St. Louis. Their home was the second home to be built on Poki Place in Diamondhead on the south side of I-10. Mario is known as the "hard-headed Spaniard" who would never evacuate for any hurricane. He had lived on the south side of Diamondhead for 14 years, had survived all previous hurricanes and felt secure in his concrete, hurricane-proof home, which was built to survive a hurricane Category 3 storm.

However, this storm was different; and their neighbor, Debbie Hussey, convinced the Espinosa's to move to the local Ramada Inn for the duration of the storm. The four reserved rooms on the bottom floor of the motel and moved here on Sunday evening. They were fortunate to have bottom floor rooms as the roof later blew off the motel, and all those staying on the top floor had to be moved downstairs where they camped in the atrium around the pool. This is one of the few motels that will allow pets. One can only imagine the commotion of all these people among the cats, dogs and parakeets.

Once the eye of the storm passed and the water receded, Mario and Max Hussey walked across I-10 to see if their homes were damaged. Much to their horror, everywhere they looked there was debris piled mile high. Walking was very difficult across downed electrical wires and nails sticking out of boards. They worked their way over and under downed trees to where their homes should be, only to find everything gone. It was a clean sweep, nothing but desolation from Airport Drive to the water. The wind, tornadoes and high water proved to be too much for even a well built home so close to the Bay of St. Louis.

As they were walking, they heard a noise, which turned out to be another neighbor, Joel Salsbury, and his friend, Robert, covered with mud, no shoes and only shorts on for clothing.

At first the men thought Joel and his friend were doing the same as they were doing, checking on their property; but they soon realized that Joel and Robert, had stayed in Joel's house through the storm and had barely survived.

Mario and Rose later recognized a few of their clothes, waving in the breeze about 60–70 feet up in the few remaining trees. They never did find any of their heavy furniture, such as sofas, reclining chairs, tables, etc., as all seemed to have disappeared off the face of the earth.

Mario's boat had been stored in a friend's airplane hangar, on the north side of Airplane Drive. The hangar had collapsed and crushed the boat inside.

Living at the Ramada Inn during the next few days proved to be very difficult without any water for showers in the oppressive heat that followed the storm. Soon, Mario, an engineer, decided to tap into the well on his property and rigged up an outdoor shower. He and some of his friends were enjoying the shower, in their birthday suits, when they suddenly heard a helicopter overhead. It was a CNN news team taking their picture.

The Espinosa and Hussey families lived together for several months before they could make other living arrangements.

Mario and Rose will rebuild, probably an all concrete home, to be built by a Vancouver, Canada, company. This home will be a showcase home, much stronger than the old home, and can sustain 300 mile per hour winds.[8]

The weeks after Katrina were the hottest days some of the locals had ever seen. Temperatures were over 98 degrees and the humidity was stifling. After a few days it cooled down to about 95 degrees. Older people do not do well in heat without air conditioning and by Tuesday the pools were full of people. This went on for 2–3 days, and the water in the pools began to look and smell bad! Signs soon warned people to keep out of the pools because of a lack of sanitation.

One woman was seen in one of the Twin Lakes, on an inner tube with a drink in her hand.

Residents were physically removing debris, first from the road in front of their homes and then from their yards. Backbreaking cleanup and construction in near–100-degree heat is a recipe for heat stroke, injury or heart attack. *"We all want our lives back to normal,"* stated one resident, however, normal had to wait; work and sacrifice had to come first.

The sewer system was only partially working, and standing water was used to flush toilets; this soon developed into a bad situation.

Golf Course Maintenance Superintendent Steve McDonald opened a community shower using an artesian well near the Twin Lake and number 15 fairway on the Cardinal Course. Joe Musacchia and Kathy Parker improved on Steve's original design so that 4–5 people could shower or wash clothes at the same time. Grass pallets were placed beneath the faucet to keep feet out of the mud and very soon, Rednecks were showering with Diamondhead millionaires. Residents arrived, carrying soap and shampoos, to shave, wash their hair or wash their underwear. Some evenings there were as many as 100 people lined up to use this facility. People could take water home; boil it for drinking or bath in it.

Communication to the outside world was terrible. Fire Chief Dennis Westbrook was the only person who had contact with the outside

The joy of cool water on a hot day at artesian well on north side of Diamondhead. The Jelinski family attempting to wash off black tar, which covered everything after the storm. (Photo by Jelinski)

world. He would travel to Waveland and return to Diamondhead with news, such as which roads were open and which ones were not.

"Information was hard to come by and not always reliable," said Chip Marz. Residents were extremely concerned about family members living elsewhere, such as Pass Christian, New Orleans or Gulfport. Diamondhead was receiving little information from the outside world and the news that did come in told of areas being wiped clean, with no one left alive. The stress was tremendous. Residents in Diamondhead thought that everyone in the Bay St. Louis and Waveland area was dead. Reports were coming in that one could not travel to the east as bridges were out on I-10, that the bridge over the River Jourdan was about to collapse. Many thought that the world, at least in the South, had been completely wiped out.

The lack of communication hampered everything. Many outside corporations were attempting to receive permission to fly into the Diamondhead airport, but they were unable to make contact with anyone. They had no way of knowing that "you just fly in—no permission needed."

However, by Thursday workers were coming into Diamondhead with cell phones that worked. Some residents were able to borrow these phones, make a call to a relative and confirm that everything was also fine. Bell South later placed telephone booths near the shopping center for residents to use, free of charge, until home phones were working.

Everyone gathered at night at the fire station to exchange news. The fire station had air conditioning! There was so much happening in Diamondhead that some volunteers did not have time to think about what was happening in the outside world. They tried to shut it out by keeping busy.

However, there were some locals who could not understand why there were no newspapers, why the post office or drug store was not open and why the country club was not serving food!

On Wednesday, Mike Collard, drove to Waveland and approached the Emergency Operations Center (EOC) and asked for generators to get the sewer department up and running again. He heard no response for 3–4 days and when he did he was asked, *"What was that you asked for?"* The department then received two generators. In the meantime, Mike had received the help he needed from the local power company. The treatment plant was partially running from day one but, under unbelievable obstacles, was fully up and running by the end of the first week

Joel Salsbury was working for the Hancock County Sheriff's Department when Katrina turned toward South Mississippi. After helping with the evacuation for several days, he chose to stay in his home in Diamondhead on the south side of I-10. Joel had built a lovely four-story home set up on piers only a year prior to the storm. He was proud that it had been featured in the Spring Pilgrimage just a few months earlier, and he was not afraid of Katrina.

His friend, Robert Abadie, decided to stay the night so Joel would not be alone. There were "no problems" all night as they sat up late playing football on the X-box before going to bed. Joel had received calls from Jodie Tate, and Robert from Inger Paine; both very concerned about the two men remaining on the coast when a Category 5 storm was approaching and wanted them to leave for safer grounds. It was very noisy as the wind was howling, and the sounds of "freight trains" were heard all night.

At 5:30 a.m. on Monday, August 29, Joel noticed water coming into his lower garage level and very quickly rising to three feet. Within thirty minutes, it had risen to six feet and Joel, in his swimming suit, was "playing" around in the water. With winds over 100 miles per hour and the waves of the water rushing around him, he was pushing away furniture and other objects from neighbors' properties that were floating into and pounding against his house. He tried to kick a refrigerator away as it rammed into him.

He went into the house to wake up Robert, who was sleeping on the second level of the home, and suggested that they go up to the third level of the house and make plans as to what to do if the water continued to rise. The wind and water were trying to break down the second floor kitchen door. Robert became very nervous. "We should not have stayed," he yelled over the howling wind.

Soon the water was nine feet high. They watched as a neighbor's house tore away from its piling, clipping Joel's house as it was being propelled through the debris by the merciless wind. Their situation was looking very serious and they agreed that they were in trouble. All the other homes around them had blown away from their pilings; the Salsbury home was the last one to hang on.

Next, the back doors broke apart and the water began rushing into the house, destroying everything in its path. They ran to the third floor where the main bedroom was located. "This house will not go down," yelled Joel, although he later admitted to feeling some doubt. Looking across the street, they could see that the power lines were down and that the water was now about 15–17 feet high. Joel walked to the back of the third floor and discovered the balconies were gone; they had been ripped off in the wind. The large glass doors across the entire wall were gone. Next, the roof blew off and, looking up, they could see the open sky.

"Now we have to go," Joel said, and they decided to swim toward a boat caught in the power lines on the street side of the house. By hanging onto parts of the house, they began to edge their way through debris toward the boat. Robert went first and made it into a boat named "Close Call." As Joel moved toward the boat, he became caught in some debris. Robert could not return to help him, and the boat was threatening to break loose from the wires holding it secure.

At approximately 11:30 a.m. the house disintegrated and began to float toward Joel in the 30–35 feet of water. This was certain danger and he began to panic. Luckily, the house brushed past on his left and floated towards the woods, where it became hung up in the trees. He managed to work himself loose from the debris and he swam toward the boat, where he was pulled in by Robert. "I can't believe this," screamed Joel. The boat tore loose from the wires that were holding it secure. It was whipped into the woods by the wind and waves. Trees were swaying and branches were breaking all around them as the boat was rammed repeatedly against the trees, until it finally became wedged and remained stable. The men were fearful that the trees would fall onto the boat and themselves.

Home of Joel Salzbury. (Photo by Baur)

It was not until the wind shifted and the worst part of the storm had passed, that Joel and Robert felt that they would live. When the water receded to about six feet deep, they decided to swim out to high ground and to the Ramada Inn where they knew they would find safety. This turned out to be a bad decision with so much debris in the water; the water was dirty, filled with broken boards and they were frightened. They swam around for about 30 minutes until they located a sailboat stuck in the woods. It had a cabin where the two men, clad only in their swimming trunks found safety from the elements. They were both in shock, their nerves on end and shivering from the cold,

Throughout the night they heard many noises such as birds, animals and something that sounded like trains or tornadoes. Thinking that they heard boats out on the Bay, they called out but no one came to their rescue. They had not had any food or water for many hours and Joel had to keep cheering Robert, who had become very melancholy. "We are alive, we made it!" Joel kept saying. Finally, they slept.

When they woke up, the water had receded and they could see the road below them. The sailboat had settled in debris and rested about two feet above the ground. They walked to Joel's garage to check out their cars and discovered that both cars had been tossed into the woods, so they began to walk towards Airport Drive. In shock and disbelief, they saw that all the homes near the shore were gone, replaced by mountains of debris. They were crawling over splintered boards, torn metal roofing and material covered with exposed nails. As they continued to walk, they pulled shirts and jackets from the trees to put on, as they were still cold. Crawling over some bushes, they saw Mario Espinosa and Max Hussey, neighbors, coming in to check their property.

As Joel and Robert walked across I-10, they met sightseers already coming to view the destruction of the south side of Diamondhead. John Bunc was one of the people who met Joel on Tuesday morning coming across the Hwy. John reports that the two men were in shock and told him that they had spent the previous night in a boat. Joel is a Reserve Deputy for Hancock County and on the Dive Team. John reported to the Hancock County Sheriff's Department Captain that he had seen Joel that morning and that he was very much alive.

They continued on to the Ramada, where they were given juice to drink. Finding someone with a cell phone, Joel made a call to his family in Baton Rouge, asking for someone to come pick him up. Trying to rest inside the building was too uncomfortable in the terrible heat, and they spent that night sleeping under the walkway outside the Inn. The next morning someone arrived to pick them up. The first thing they did after arriving in Baton Rouge was go to the mall and purchase clothes as they did not even have shoes to wear.

Joel says that all during the storm he never felt as though he was going to die. As a scuba diver, he has no fear of the water, and he believes that he could have saved himself by swimming. "It was like making a pre-made movie without reality." He does not plan to rebuild on his lot in Diamondhead but will clear the lot, pour a slab and put a "For Sale" sign on it.[9]

Mississippi Forgotten

Just as the "big time media" forgot most of the nation during the Civil War and reported everything happening in Virginia, the same happened after Katrina in South Mississippi. The late author and historian, Shelby Foote, said of the Civil War: "The whole damn war wasn't fought in Virginia…, but because the photographers and reporters were there, Virginia got the play in the big-time newspapers."[10]

Once again, the reporters and the "big-time" media could not get past New Orleans. The "Big E" did suffer a tremendous tragedy that needed to be told, but so did South Mississippi. To ignore the full scope of destruction of Katrina was not telling the whole story.

The awful tragedy that fell on New Orleans the day after Katrina hit the coast will be a compelling saga of politics and abuse for many years to come. This city became "The Story" and held the national media spellbound for weeks as it covered the plight of poor people trapped on rooftops, held captive without food or water in terrible shelters and finally made their journey to unknown places.

If the levees had not broken, there would have been no New Orleans story to report. New Orleans was not a Katrina story but was reported as a Levee Board story of political incompetence, coupled with state government incompetence.

It is obvious to anyone who follows the national news that the number of news stories on New Orleans was many times that of those focused on the Coast.

In the shadows of the New Orleans story, the Mississippi Gulf Coast had become invisible and forgotten to most Americans. The story of the missing Alabama teenager received more coverage on most cable networks than all of the incredibly compelling stories of courage, loss and needs of untold thousands of Mississippians.

To many Northerners, Katrina happened in Louisiana, not along the Gulf Coast. Months later a service provider commented to a local, "I never heard a thing about Diamondhead after the storm on the radio or TV; you have major damage here."

Most people have no idea how much destruction there was from the storm and how long it will be before anything looks natural again along the Mississippi Coast. Even though help from around the country was overwhelming, Americans are known to have a remarkably short attention span.

The depth of suffering and the height of the destruction in Mississippi reveal incredible stories that American people should know about. The Mississippi Coast was seldom mentioned during those terrible days following Katrina, and, if mentioned, then only as an add-on paragraph that would briefly reveal what was taking place there. Television trucks were seen for a short time after the storm and then nothing. After about six months, some stations began reporting from some of the devastated areas, but those programs were not well advertised, and northerners were now not interested. They believed and still believe that the Coast is "all fixed up again."

The Charles Corey family, living on Anela Place, stayed for the storm. Charles, his mother and a son, Scott were home that morning when Katrina arrived. Early in the morning, a neighbor, whose house was lower than the Corey home, had walked up to the Corey home to ask if he could move his car to the higher area, as water was coming into his carport. Before long water was also reaching the Corey home, considerably higher in elevation, and was soon up to the top of the windows. Some of these people ended up standing on the kitchen table, and some out on the roof before the storm passed and the water began to recede. That night the Baptist Church became their refuge for dry clothes, food and a dry place to rest their heads.

Charles said that immediately the next day mold began to develop on everything. Because he was able to wash his house off right away with a hose he was able to save many of his valuables and furniture.

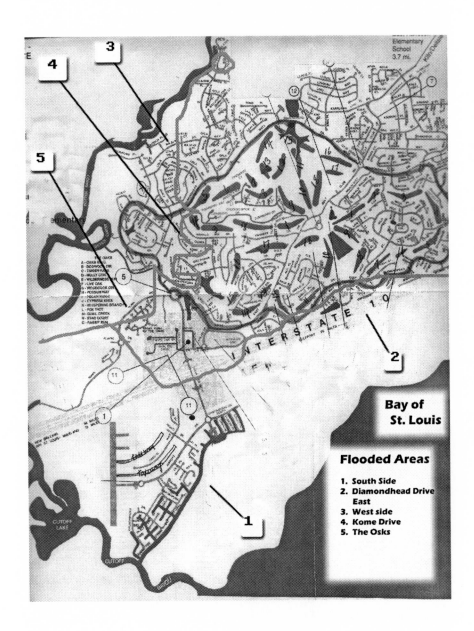

Trouble

M ike Collard, Manager of the Water and Sewer Departments, had
taken his family away for the storm. After grabbing a few hours of
sleep he drove back to Diamondhead during the storm. The interstate
was under water near the 603 exit and power lines lay across the highway about two feet off the road, making driving very precarious. He
arrived at Diamondhead about 1 p.m. With so many trees and wires
down over the streets, getting to the maintenance facility, where the
water well was located, was tricky. The wastewater treatment plant had
received 15 feet of salt water. After getting a generator working, he
jumped on a backhoe tractor, made a loop trip around the community to
check on the water tower and attempted to get the water system up and
running. He found that 18 lift stations were now under salt water.

The water tower was empty of water and the department has
never been able to determine exactly why. Had the power been off long
enough for the remaining few residents left in Diamondhead to drain
the tower, or was it something else that did it? It was a miracle that the
tower stood during the storm because it was empty during the high
winds.

Mike went to the fire station to discuss with Chief Westbrook
what should be done first. They decided that it was critical to get water
to the Fire station, the Community Center, The Baptist Church, where
the refugees were housed and fed, and to Woodland Village Nursing
Home.

One water and sewer employee showed up to work; and they
began work by isolating some of the water lines, keeping only one open
as the tower was not filling up as it should be. They began to check for
leaks. After about 4 days, it was discovered that all of the water hydrants
in Lanai Village had been opened. Once these were shut off, the tower

quickly filled with water and residents began to receive water into their homes.

This problem had caused a great delay in getting the water back up for residents. "There were many citizens who thought they knew better than the authorities and only hindered the operations of each department," said Chief Westbrook. "All of this created frustration on everyone's part and took double the time to restore facilities that it should have."

At first the water received in homes was intermittent as the department was afraid of running out of diesel fuel, which was needed to operate the generators. Within ten days Diamondhead had water service to all livable homes.

The wastewater treatment center was filled with debris such as home columns, siding, etc. and had to be manually cleaned of this mess. The treatment plant was partially operating from day one and fully up and running by the end of the first week. "During those first few critical days, every POA employee made every step count and soon facilities were up and running under unbelievable obstacles," said Mike.[11]

Almost as soon as the storm had passed, the looters were out. Several looters were confronted by a local resident and his shotgun, and soon scampered off.

People began stealing gas at gunpoint. To head out on a back road was treacherous. One person pulled a knife while standing in line for gas in Diamondhead. The next day men from the Mississippi Bureau of Investigation arrived to help control the situation. They arrived with control vests and billy clubs, and they were big! The gas lines then became orderly.

People were frightened because there were many strangers around Diamondhead. People were walking in off the interstate, going to the flooded areas and looting homes. Some were simply looking for work, some for a place of refuge.

Al and Barbara Hermann, Hancock County Sheriff Deputies, worked tirelessly to handle the numerous reports of looting. Together they raided two homes where $6,000 of looted valuables were recovered and suspects arrested! Diamondhead's security force, under Reggie Fayard, burned the candle at both ends, working both traffic and patrol details.

One resident on the north side of Diamondhead was using a generator when he noticed someone running with it to his truck. He grabbed a shotgun, which was sitting beside his door, raised the gun and yelled,

"Hey, you take one more step and I will shoot you." The person dropped the generator, jumped in his truck and took off.

For three and four days, there was no law and order in Diamondhead. Security was getting to be a problem. Someone stole gasoline that was needed to run the Baptist Church generators to keep food from spoiling. People were caught looting the condominium area south of the highway, and soon no one was allowed to enter that area unless that person could prove that he lived there. A few residents from the north side of Diamondhead insisted on getting into the south area. One police officer was almost run over by someone insisting that he was going in, no matter what the ruling was.

On Wednesday Diamondhead residents were taking shifts, all armed, around the front entrance. Anyone attempting to enter Diamondhead off the interstate was told that no gas, food or drugs were available.

The police discovered that most complaints were not actually from looting, but something else. Many turned out to be residents searching through debris, which had been placed near the street for pickup. Nights were dark and very scary as there were no lights of any kind. A curfew was set for everyone. No one was allowed on the streets from 6 p.m. until 6 a.m.

By Wednesday, stories of looting, shootings and disorder in New Orleans were spreading to Diamondhead, and many were concerned that the same could happen in Diamondhead. People became very frightened, causing tension for many.

Horror stories were circulating everywhere, from bodies being removed from trees in the Devil's Elbow area to hundreds of dead bodies on the south side. The stories became bigger and bigger with a murder in Diamondhead, rape at the Ramada Inn, and the death of a three-year-old child during the storm.

Shannon Dye told this story first hand to Dr. Patricia Collier:

Diamondhead security picked up a man who had been beaten up. While bandaging him, Shannon asked what happened. The guy told him that he had been caught looting in Diamondhead and a guardsmen beat him up, drove him to the Louisiana border, slowed down and threw him out of the car. He then complained that he bad to walk all the way back to Diamondhead. Shannon said that all he could do was shake his head at the stupidity of the man—actually admitting that he had been caught looting and then walking back to the same area.

At the Ramada Inn, things were ugly and totally out of control. The Inn had a tough group of men who had checked in before the storm and refused to leave.

A young woman, her mother and her small child asked for refuge at the church, as they were too frightened to remain at the inn. She said that people were pushing her room door open, walking through the room and using her bathroom.

Then, the call came on Wednesday evening about 8:30 p.m., "The Calvary has arrived!" Chip Marz drove to the interstate interchange, where he was greeted by 30 Alabama State Trooper vehicles, all with lights flashing and two troopers in each car. "What a relief," said Chip.

"What can we do?" asked one. Immediately, one group was sent to clean out the problems at the Ramada Inn. The others were to cover the three entrances of Diamondhead, the main gate, the south side and the north entrance. "I want you to be seen; patrol these streets with your lights on and attempt to relieve the minds of the residents so they can stop worrying about looters," said the fire chief.

Diamondhead was locked tightly down that night. A huge weight had been lifted from many shoulders, and residents began to feel secure once again. Diamondhead was not able to keep all of these troopers, as they had to be shared with other towns around the area, but a few remained here.

The week after Katrina hit, Harrison County had 1,000 people in the county jail. The building had no water, air conditioning or toilets, however, the Warden said, "Bring me the looters, I will find an inch of room somewhere to put them. They must be contained." [12]

Andy and Tonya Perniciaro who had evacuated, returned on Tuesday and found what was left of their house on Anoi Way was in better condition than many other homes on their street; however, it was heartbreaking. The huge amount of water had left most of the roof, but one-half of the walls had washed away.

All of their furniture, along with some items that they were storing for someone else, was scattered, helter-skelter, throughout the neighborhood. Other peoples' belongings were found inside their home and around their yard.

They discovered wild boars, some very large in size, and some baby boars in their house and in the surrounding area. They found raccoons in their yard and many dead birds. [13]

Oaks photo (Photo by Gremillion)

Mrs. Pugh came to the Baptist Church, desperate to find someone who could help convince her husband that it was impossible to save anything from their home on the East side of Diamondhead. Her husband had a heart condition and the heat was unbearable. Mr. Pugh wanted to salvage as much as possible from his house, but the structure was not sound. Bill & Curt Dye were able to convince him to stop going into the house, as he was risking his life. Bill removed Mr. Pugh's hard drives so that he could try to salvage some of his computer business.[14]

Wendell Sanderson Jr., his wife, Elizabeth, Kelsie 8, Jamie 12 and Ericka 16 lived very close to I-10 on the east side of Diamondhead. On the day that Katrina struck, the family was watching the storm from inside their house. All of the trees in their back yard had fallen over, all toward the west. Erika opened the back door and the water began to pour over her. It was difficult to get the door closed again. They decided to begin removing items from the floor and setting them on taller furniture. The two dogs and two cats were placed on a three-foot high brick divider wall. The water was getting higher and the refrigerator began to float around the kitchen. Shoes and other small items were floating all over the house. The water kept rising and the animals were moved to the attic.

After everyone was safely up in the attic, Elizabeth fell through the floor, catching herself in time to pull herself back up. Several calls were made to 911 from a cell phone but were always disconnected. No call ever got through to the fire station, where rescue might be available.

The sidewall of the house to the east collapsed in and everyone was moved out onto the roof. The wind was blowing very hard and soon the roof collapsed. Everyone went down with it but it settled into a flat position broken into four sections. The decision was made to move to another section than the one they were on. To accomplish this they had to jump from one section to the other. Most of the family jumped to safety but the first section moved in the water and Elizabeth fell into the water as she jumped. She was pulled to safety by her husband.

The family remained on the roof for at least four hours. All during that time rain continued to pelt them with what felt like hail. They were sitting in about four feet of water and the wind was hurling many items into them, creating numerous cuts and bruises. Ericka was hit in the head by an industrial mop pail.

They watched the pine tree to the west of the house, bending in the wind and almost touching them, fearful that it would break off and kill them. They grabbed at items that might float, as they blew past them, hoping that something might help keep them afloat if they ended up in the water and had to save themselves from drowning.

They watched the wind reverse, and slowly, very slowly, the water began to go down. When they felt it was low enough, they stepped from the roof, directly onto their driveway. The house had collapsed almost to the ground.

They were able to make their way up the street and take refuge in someone's garage. In the meantime, Wendell's son made his way from the north end of Diamondhead to their home; finding the house on the ground and no one around, he feared the worst. He made his way to the Baptist Church, where he told everyone that the family had perished in the collapsed home. Several hours later the family met up to confirm that they were fine, just very shook up and beat up. One dog did not make it to safety; the other three animals survived.

Wendell and Elizabeth both have frequent nightmares about those hours spent on the collapsed roof of their home. Elizabeth's dreams all end in everyone perishing during that frightful time.[15]

The five homes that collapsed on Alki Way were occupied by: from the left end—a family that had left for the storm; the Sandersons, who rented; two empty rental homes and the Bill Dye home.

East side homes collapse. (Photo by author)

Home of Bill Dye. (Photo by author)

To The Rescue

Within a few days, the Baptist Church in Diamondhead assumed the role of sole refugee center and began preparing three meals a day for an ever-growing number of area residents. Everyone volunteering was working very long hours.

POA Club Manager Jeff Hall and his staff took over the meal operation. The food from the Country Club was hauled to the Baptist Church, along with the freezers, which were kept operating with generators. Paper plates, etc. were obtained from the grocery store. The Country Club staff was doing the cooking on grills, kept going with donated propane tanks from people's homes. The POA later purchased $8,000 worth of food, which was brought in by an 18-wheeler to continue the food service. There was a big need for dog and cat food, as many people had fled their homes with their pets, but there was no food for them.

Dr. Patricia Collier, who was Minister of Music at the Baptist Church in Diamondhead during Katrina recalls:

A total of 49 people camped out in the Baptist church buildings during the storm. The new church addition had been built with very strong cement walls, able to stand a very bad hurricane. Everyone slept very little on Sunday night, as we constantly heard the roar of freight trains, which was really the sound of tornados. Every time I tried to sleep I was again woke by that horrible sound. On Monday morning the water began to come through the seal of the front doors which kept many occupants busy mopping up water. The doors had to be kept locked because the wind kept forcing them open.

We moved to the basement area of the new building about 9 a.m., to shelter from the possibility of a tornado hitting the building. Then the word came to us about 9:15 that water was rising very fast outside and we needed to come back upstairs.

At 9:45 a.m., on Monday morning, the water began to enter the basement area and rose so fast we could hardly clear the floor of the few things we had stored there.

Watching the storm through the front windows, we were stunned to see a lake appear all around us. Now the little amount of water coming in through the doors did not seem so important. From the trees on the west side of the church all the way to Clayton Marshall's house on Diamondhead Drive North was a solid lake of water. Someone noticed a deer swimming past the church.

Water rushing past the Baptist Church at Diamondhead during the storm. (Photo by Courmier)

The pines were almost bending over to the ground. The stately old oak tree in front of the church did not bend with the wind, remained standing. It gradually kept losing branches and leaves until it was bare. At about 12:15 p.m., the eye of Katrina must have passed as the wind began to reverse in direction. After the storm, we felt lucky, as the church had sustained very little damage. We had about 8 inches of water in the basement, which was still unfinished and easy to clean, but the outside wall showed a water line of 36 inches.

A few of our people decided to leave about 3 p.m. to check out their homes. Some soon returned because they could not get through the downed power lines and trees blocking the streets.

About 3:30 p.m., the Charles Corey family walked in, soaking wet, scared and happy to have some shelter. This was the first family seeking shelter and the first we knew that homes had been flooded.

About 5:30 p.m., another family arrived at the church seeking shelter and we now realized that we might have to shelter and clothe many families. We began to prepare for what we knew was coming, as we knew many of our parishioners were in the flooded area. How should we do this? It was first decided to write down their names and put the people in the old sanctuary room. We passed out t-shirts, to these soaking wet people, from the Resource Room, We were soon overwhelmed by people walking into the church, seeking refuge and looking so lost and desolate.

How were we going to feed this amount of people? It was decided that someone should leave and find out if the grocery store was open. After finding the store closed, they noticed people carrying cakes out of the Dairy Queen. The owner was informed of the refugees at the church and the lack of food to feed them. She began to have our truck loaded with hamburgers, hotdogs, chicken, breakfast sausages, ham, cheese and ice cream. Everything that was in the Dairy Queen's freezers was loaded and brought to the Baptist Church to serve the over 100 people who were staying there. This was enough to feed everyone for supper and breakfast the next day. There was so much to do that night that most of us did not sleep that night either.

There was a barbecue grill at the church that was used to cook this food. We even learned how to do French fries and biscuits on a gas grill. Everything was possible if we tried.

By now we had generators hooked up to the refrigerators, coffee makers brewing coffee and a few went home to get more grills to cook on. Propane tanks were obtained from the Wal-Mart in Waveland. However, we had no dry clothes for these poor wet people. Many of us went home and brought back whatever we could find and attempted to clothe these people.

We now knew that sections in Diamondhead south of I-10, one area on the east side and many streets on the west side along Diamondhead North were gone or badly damaged. Here is where many of our parishioners lived. So many were now beginning to learn about what they had really lost. The mementos from a lifetime were now gone. Like there was nothing to help remember those lost years.

By Tuesday night we had people in every corner of the building for a total of 124 people. Refugees from the Episcopal Church and the Community Center were now moved to our facility. We had received a few supplies from the Wal-Mart Store in Waveland where one of our members worked.

On Wednesday rules were laid down for those staying in our facilities. All pets had to be moved to the north breezeway and all dogs had to remain on leashes and the cats in carriers. I was able to get a short phone call out that day to an aunt of mine to let my family know I was O.K.

By now "hot and sweaty" was the attire for all of us. No one could take a shower or clean up as there was no water. We moved a large bulletin board to the Fellowship Center where telephone numbers could be posted. The most important part of the board for most refugees was the present date, which was updated every day.

Wednesday evening we had a prayer service. It was very hard for me to choose appropriate songs because most songs consisted of the words such as, "When upon life's billows you are tempest tossed, when you are discouraged thinking all is lost." Here were people who had literally been tossed by the billows and lost everything. These people were just thankful to be alive and too concerned at this time about immediate needs such as food, shelter and water.

Supplies were now running very low and we had seen no sign of any aid except for a small amount of water and ice. After acquiring some pool water to wash some of the grime off of my face, I went to bed that night in my own home praying that I could sleep. My next-door neighbor was sitting on his front porch with a shotgun on his lap, ready to fend off looters.

On Thursday morning I drove back to the church at 5 miles per hour, which was the fastest that I could move. After breakfast was served, someone told us that we should drive to the Dollar General in Bay St. Louis where we could find needed supplies.

I drove down the Interstate dodging recliners, broken tree branches and boats. There were no traffic lights working. My first sight of the gas stations on 603 was stupefying. The three gas stations on the corner of 603 were destroyed and mud covered everything. A truck was scraping mud from the northbound lane, as if it was snow.

Taken by a cell phone, looking south from the bridge on the corner of Hwy 603 and I-10, shortly after the storm. Water was about 35 feet at this intersection and was now receding. (Photo by Tate)

All along 603 the damage was very evident. There was debris—large debris piles along the road including power poles and lines. The new shopping center on the west side of the road was completely destroyed; it looked like shredded metal. There were huge trailers lying sideways and there were hundreds of cars that usually line 603 for all approaching storms in the ditches, with either their tail or noses down. When I got closer to Hwy 90, some of the fish cabins, from the east side of the road, were now on the west side of the road. Three boats were swamped together in one bayou.

As I got closer to Sue Favre's house, I tried to look for it; I could see that it had no stairs and no roof, and the house was easy to see because some of the trees that usually hid it were gone. All I could do was shake my head in disbelief.

At DeRussy's, cars were everywhere—even through the plate glass windows, piled one on top of each other.

As I was driving down highway 90 toward the east, I noticed some businesses appeared to be fine on the outside, but the broken windows, missing doors and dipping roofs told a different story. When I got to the EMS, people loaded my car to the brink, at the Dollar General Store, and even strapped a few cases of supplies, to the top, with belts. This included plates, trash bags, cups, socks, tents, feminine products, diapers, paper towels, cleaners, etc.

I came back on Longfellow Road and noticed the new apartments had all been flooded and the Hancock County Civic Center was destroyed. (It has since been bulldozed). All of this area had taken a high amount of water. Trucks were working on replacing power poles.

Approaching the 603 overpass, I could see the debris line only one foot from the top of the bridge. All the grass along the highway was dead and many pine trees and shrubs hit by the salt water. Crossing the Jourdan River Bridge I looked to my right and noticed that there were only pilings where I knew there should be beautiful homes. At the Diamondhead exit I saw the damage to the Ace Hardware and a glimpse of the Yacht Club, which was now an open-air restaurant.

When I returned for a second load, accompanied by the Lakeys, the Dollar General store was now cordoned off by a Florida Sheriff. He said that we could load only what was outside of the store and that we could not go back in and get anything from inside. We loaded up the back of my pickup with cereal—we filled it with cereal. Canned goods, candy, drinks, water, etc. went into the back of the Lakey's pick up and both cabs. I left my name and address with the sheriff. I laughingly refer to this as the day my name was put on a sheriff's report for looting.

Horror stories were everywhere. One parishioner had to use a ladder to check out the damage inside his home. Many families had lost everything. I became deeply affected by these poor people who had received as much as 12 feet of water in their homes, when I had escaped with only a few missing shingles. These were people that I cared for, but

I had no power to help them. All I could do was cry for them, because as of yet, they had no tears.

The only aid we seemed to be getting was the water and ice that our fire department had acquired from Waveland and the few businesses that had donated or provided food. Some of the local businesses that had provided for us were Dairy Queen, Subway, Diamondhead Discount Drug, Diamondhead Country Club, Diamondhead Grocery, Wal-Mart, Dollar General and many local citizens with freezers of food.

Other than that Diamondhead was taking care of its own.

On Thursday, we had one of the greatest surprises in store for all of us. Mark Carpenter of Gladewater, Texas arrived with a trailer loaded with generators, gasoline, clothes and food, but most of all the knowledge that the outside world knew that Diamondhead, Mississippi needed help. In addition, to this gesture he restored hope to many of us who were wondering if anyone outside of this area even knew we still existed.

The POA was as busy as the rest of us, but its duties included dealing with Diamondhead Water & Sewer, Coast Electric, getting the roads cleared, etc.

By this time we were getting the feeding of meals and distribution down to a science. We were learning as we worked, and were becoming accustomed to the long hot hours of each day.

Julie was busy with another nurse keeping most health concerns under control. Russell Love opened the pharmacy with a doctor to provide Rx for those with chronic illnesses or daily medications. Susan was overseeing the food pantry. I was keeping in touch with the Fire Department and helping where I could, mostly in the kitchen.

We were now under a curfew from 6 p.m. to 6 a.m. and we had to have dinner finished before six, but we workers could not leave the church until at least seven.

Friday, September 2, 2005

By this time, I was becoming extremely exhausted; Friday and Saturday are a blur. The main thing I remember about Friday is that I helped cook lunch at the grills and almost suffered heat stroke. All I wanted was to wash my hair. I had not had anything more than a cold sponge bath since Sunday before the storm.

The kitchen sink at the church now had flowing water. I found a bottle of baby shampoo and I washed my hair in the kitchen sink! It was as if God said, "Here, have a little comfort." I was so happy and felt so good that someone mentioned the new spring in my step and that I had discovered a hidden fount of energy.

We had several truck loads of food arrive that day, clothing, bottled water, canned foods, etc., all donated from somewhere around the country.

The locals taking refuge in the church were slowly beginning to make contact with family members from outside the area. Some were accepting the fact that their lives were changed forever. As people began to leave our little sheltered existence, our tensions became more evident, because those leaving had been the greatest help of all.

I told Dr. Warren about the pastor in Gantt that wanted to send in a team of volunteers. I was given the go ahead to contact him and let him know about our needs. They were the first team to provide aid in Diamondhead, outside of a government agency, after the truck from Texas.

I now had running water at my home, albeit contaminated, but good enough to take a cold shower. I do not remember much about Saturday—the days were becoming all alike. Get up, go to church, cook, sweat, cook some more, clean, sweat some more, cook, sweat.... We were slowly becoming robots—stinky robots.

During the service on Sunday, September 4, 2005, I sang, "Saved by Grace." I was able to sing a little stronger than normal because the words echoed what all of us were feeling, that God had truly saved us by His grace

That day we moved the meal serving process into the Methodist Church facilities, as they had gas stoves, ovens and the room to serve large crowds. We were now able to provide basic necessities and formed a food and supply pantry at the Baptist Church as truckloads of supplies were beginning to arrive.

Traveling through Texas on Tuesday, September 6, 2005, I was visiting with a waiter and he asked where we were from. When we told him South Mississippi, he asked how it was here, because all he was seeing on TV was New Orleans. I told him about the flooding and destruction to Diamondhead, Bay St. Louis and Waveland. He had seen a small item about Pass Christian, but had no idea that the destruction along the coast was as bad as it was. As it turned out no one did! The national news media was focusing on the flooding of New Orleans; the Mississippi Gulf Coast was an after thought.

As we drove on to Texas we met numerous National Guard and power trucks from Arizona and New Mexico and trucks loaded with bobcats and power poles. I was heartened by the number of trucks carrying supplies into South Mississippi.

Some members of the church, who had been flooded out, remained in the church building until about mid September. Those staying there were encouraged to go back and begin to work on their homes. We knew that as long as they stayed at the church they would make no headway on getting their lives back together. They had to move on and sooner would be better than later.

We were still giving out water until October. The Baptist Church had now become a distribution center for the surrounding area. We were handing out food and necessary items to people from the Kiln, Pass Christian, Waveland and Bay St. Louis. At Christmas, we had oodles of toys available to give out for the entire county. Thousands of packages were handed out to children.

When we stopped being a distribution center, donations were still coming in from all over the nation and we would then deliver to wherever they were needed.[16]

Volunteers were needed for a variety of jobs: traffic control, food, water, ice distribution and refugee assistance. Volunteer, Norman Parker, recruited and coordinated other volunteers, including his wife, Janet, who worked in several capacities. People just "showed up" at the churches to volunteer. It was only due to the wonderful volunteers who made things happen that anything operated at all. Immediately, the community began to organize pick up groups. Volunteers were soon picking up debris, spearing paper, signs, shingles, roofing nails, branches and all kinds of garbage.

"The teenagers were wonderful!" said Chief Westbrook They did lots of running between the station house and water lines, etc. Those working outside in the stifling weather were working in horrible conditions. One teenage volunteer working the lines had to be treated for heat exhaustion.

On Wednesday Merrill Lynch flew in a plane with food and chain saws. Thursday a bit more ice arrived, which was gone in ten minutes. At 8 a.m. there were 100 cars parked in line waiting for ice and water. Supply lines moved from the B.P. gas station to the fire station lot and then to the main parking lot near the grocery store.

The BP gas station opened on Thursday with some gas available. The line of cars was fast to form and miles long. Rumors arose that gas had not arrived because FEMA had hi-jacked the trucks for their own use. The Chevron station opened to sell snack foods and cigarettes, and the lines were long there also, but no gas was available.

Other fire departments from Florida and one from Northern Mississippi began arriving with their trucks to relieve local firemen, who had been working for five days straight. They were allowed to go home to check on their families and property. The relief crews were housed at the fire department building.

By Thursday evening, September 2, ninety percent of the Diamondhead roads had been cleared. That day Hancock County moved their equipment into Diamondhead and took over the road clearing duties. The County widened and cleared the remaining streets.

Power and phone crews arrived to help from many states. North Carolina, New Hampshire and Alabama crews and others, worked day and night to restore power to thousands of homes and businesses. Many

Some homes were not completely washed away on the south side of Diamondhead. (Photo by Baur)

people lost appliances as power surges went on and off, damaging even new products.

Some areas had power by Thursday and after two weeks all homes in Diamondhead that could be hooked up had electricity. After about five days, Diamondhead began to acquire a "trickle" of water and people were so appreciative of this small gain.

The nursing home owner, Ted Caine, requested help in moving

his people to Hattiesburg. Without electricity, it was impossible to adequately care for them. Volunteers rounded up several Hancock County School buses, and several loads of patients were soon transported to Hattiesburg.

Chief Westbrook said, "Things were very hectic during those first few days; but to the rescue came Stormy Wyman, who volunteered to cook for the crew. She was at the fire department on the first day after the storm and remained for about two weeks. The men would grab something to eat in the morning and not return until dark. "She was a great cook!" said one of the crew, "and a lifesaver."

Several nurses were staying in the fire station, helping out. Medical groups from various areas around the U.S. assisted the local doctors at the Hancock Family Medical Center near the front entrance of Diamondhead. One E.R. nurse from Maine remained for one month. All service was free for the first month.

According to those who remained for the next week after Katrina, *life was tough.* There was no water, food, gas, electricity or telephones and it was *Hot!*

Linda Baur and her 14-year old collie, Nancy, moved from Maine to her new home on Timber Park in the Oaks area of Diamondhead in July, just a few days before Hurricane Dennis turned into the Gulf. In late August, when Katrina was entering the Gulf of Mexico, Linda's floors were still covered with boxes of books, old records, dishes and kitchen equipment she had yet to unpack. Potted palms and unplanted shrubs in pots joined the clutter.

On Monday morning, still in her pajamas, Linda passed the time by snapping photos of the storm through her window, petting and reassuring Nancy as she watched a large branch in a nearby pine swing like a pendulum in the wind. Despite hearing tree branches hitting her roof during the night, no trees had yet posed a danger to the house. She was irritated rather than frightened when water from broken window seals began to puddle in her bedroom.

Sitting on the floor, watching the storm outside, she noticed that the puddles of rainwater had now turned into a sheet of wind-swept water. Suddenly, it began leaking under the door and soaking the carpet. Still assuming the water was only drainage overflow, Linda started hoisting boxes of books onto her sofa. The water continued to rise and the boxes began to float. She waded in water to her bedroom hoping to rescue her photograph albums.

When Linda heard her refrigerator crash in the kitchen, she turned to see Nancy standing helpless and bewildered in water up to her neck. "I realized then that we were in real trouble and being from the North I had no clue as to what I should do." She put Nancy on the floating bed and placed her computer on a high, kitchen cabinet shelf. "I waded from room to room looking for what I most wanted to save. I found my camera, with its now precious storm photos, submerged in four feet of water. At some point, I became spooked by the underwater glow of a battery-operated hurricane lamp," said Linda.

When the water was about one foot from the top of the windows, she grabbed her purse and unable to open the doors, cut a hole in the screen of a window and climbed out. "I left Nancy on the bed without saying 'goodbye' because she appeared to be asleep with hopes that she would float safely until I could come back for her," Linda recalls with tears in her eyes.

Using the gutters to hang onto, she moved across the front of the house to her carport, where she stopped to rest on top of her car, pondering what to do next. When water topped the car, she swam to the backyard privacy fence. Hanging onto the fence and a gutter drainpipe with debris swirling into her back, her eyes searched for calmer water and protective trees that she could reach. "It was like being in my own episode of *Storm Stories*, like reading an exciting book," said Linda. But, this was a *real* story—my own story—after awhile I just wanted to find a quiet place to rest and pretend this was not happening to me."

When the water reached the fence top, she left her relative security and swam to a downed tree midway between the homes of the next cul-de-sac. These homes were on higher ground and the water appeared to be less deep. "Heading into "open water" with swift currents, and not being a strong swimmer, was scary for me. I made it to the tree, rested for a while and then began swimming towards another house. When I was able to touch ground, I knew I had made it."

Sitting on the front steps of a stranger's home, Linda wondered if she dared break into the house. She needed dry clothes and shelter from the cold. She was clad only in her nightgown and the air had turned to freezing cold. Suddenly a man stuck his head out of a hurricane hole of another house with most of its roof blown away. She shouted to him and he invited her into that home and found her some dry clothes. It was Dan Ellis, local historian and author, who was house-sitting. Waiting out the storm, he began telling her stories of Hurricane Camille. He explained

First look at Linda Baur's living room after 6 feet of water.
(Photo by Baur)

that Diamondhead remained dry during that storm in '69. She asked him to please go to her house and check on her dog that she had left behind on the bed. He did go over and look but could not find Nancy.

Mike Picnot, who lived up the street, invited her to stay with his family for a few days before she was able to find permanent housing. His home had a generator, food, dry clothes and no floodwater. Linda's dog, Nancy, was later found dead in her home.

Linda is a smoker and being caught without any cigarettes and under so much stress was highly uncomfortable for her. She was obliged to rely on cigars that Dan Ellis offered her. For three days, Linda was seen roaming the Oaks area with a large sized cigar in her mouth.

"During those months after the storm, I met many survivors and rescuers, who have become my very good friends. I owe my return to normalcy to the author of this book," she relates.[17]

Al and Lou Revell, live at One Rabbit Run in the Oaks Village of Diamondhead. Originally, from California, the couple had lived in their home for only one year when Katrina hit the coast. Unfamiliar with hurricanes, Lou called 911 when the water began to come into their home. When told that they had no responders available at that time, she asked, "What can we do? My husband is crippled and does not swim." The reply was, "Get up in your attic—and take something sharp with you in case you have to cut your way out to the roof."

The entrance to the attic was a two-foot square hole, high in the bedroom closet ceiling with no drop down ladder. Running to the kitchen for a tool of some sort and finding the refrigerator blocking the doorway, Lou pushed the refrigerator aside and found the drawers all under water. Feeling around in the knife drawer, she grabbed two sturdy knives and a battery radio, flashlight and some water. They hustled to get a cat, a dog and themselves into the attic. A kitchen chair was placed under the opening, but it kept floating away because the water was now about three feet deep. Al was standing in water up to his chin when he managed to climb onto a shelf in the closet and with her help was able to get into the attic. "I am crippled and cannot swim. It is amazing what one can do when water is threatening to cover your head. We barely made it up there," said Al.

The water rose to a height of six feet in their home, then stopped and began to recede. Looking out of the attic vent, Al saw a neighbor, who had floated on a board over to the Revell home to check on them. The water left within about 30 minutes and they were able to come down to what Katrina had left them. The water was gone, but the carpets held moisture and they sloshed across them as they attempted to pick up furniture strewn helter skelter around the rooms. Some items had rammed into the walls, leaving large holes.

Neighbors arrived to help lift the heavy furniture and place it where it should have been. The animals would lift their feet high in the air when they walked across the carpet, as they hated the wetness.

Al and Lou spent the next three days in the house until their son could come and get them. They left to spend two weeks in California, but they returned to face the music of cleaning up the mess. As they walked into the house, their discovered two inches of green mold on the once gold colored sofa. Practically everything in the house was covered in mold. What were they to do and where were they to start?

It was suggested they go to the Baptist Church and ask for help. When they arrived, they met about ten young men in the parking lot who told them that they were in Diamondhead to do volunteer work. They were planning to cut trees, etc.; but the person in charge of giving out jobs told them that they had nothing for them to do at the time.

After the couple registered for help, they returned to their home; shortly, the group of men from Tennessee showed up and offered their help. They represented a Baptist Church in Franklin, Tennessee. Soon they had stripped everything from the soaked and rotting Revell home. Carpet, sheetrock and furniture were taken to the street for pick up.

The men returned the next day and told the couple, "We have been talking and praying over this and have decided to adopt you. We will return each weekend and work in your home until it is back to normal."

"What will we owe you?" asked Al. "Absolutely nothing," one replied.

For five weekends, with a nine-hour road trip each way, the men returned pulling trailers loaded with supplies. They began working in the home, replacing windows, doors, kitchen cupboards, etc. They even rebuilt the closets. The Revells had only to update the electrical and plumbing, buy carpeting and pay to mud the sheetrock. One of the men had a friend who was a carpenter living in Florida. When he learned of this project, he said, "I am tearing all of the appliances out of a spec home right now. They are only one year old and I will send them to Diamondhead for you to install in the Revell home."

Then the carpenter sent a crew of 5–6 from Florida to paint everything in the house. There were extra supplies for some of the neighbors. The Revells son provided some of their furniture, but the crew from Tennessee also delivered furniture.

Al Revell replied, "Next storm, I am going to leave!"

Five Days After Katrina

At first the arrival of supplies was very sporadic. There were not enough provisions coming in to supply the needy during the first week. Many people had to be turned away.

One could not predict exactly the time any trucks would deliver. On Friday, Diamondhead received both water and ice and was informed that no more supplies would be delivered for at least 48 hours. Signs were put out to discourage the people from getting in line. By 8 a.m., Saturday, the line had already formed and when told that they would not receive anything before Monday, they argued that they were not giving up their place in line. Moreover, to everyone's surprise, at 9 a.m. a truck showed up. A few MRE's were on this truck. Everything was gone in thirty minutes.

The system of keeping everyone in their cars and not letting anyone outside their vehicle while in line, turned out to be a wonderful solution to problems that other towns were not solving. In Waveland, people had to get out of their cars and get into a long line to receive supplies, and they had to have something to place them in. In the unbearable heat, people were soon pushing and causing all sorts of problems.

On Friday evening, cars lined up for gas, stretched from the Diamondhead Realty Office to the Texaco Station on the south side of the highway. At one point a local radio station had announced, (no one ever knew where it received this information) that there was gas available to purchase at Diamondhead. Word had spread throughout the county and within an hour there were lines of cars coming in from the highway looking for gas. However, there was no gas available for them at Diamondhead. People desperately needed gas for their generators to save the food in their freezers and to fill their cars. In addition, people wanting to leave the area were trapped without gas.

When gas ran out after some had waited in line for hours, they slept in their cars, waiting for the gas trucks to arrive and refill the tanks.

By the end of the first week, it was impossible to keep the Interstate open in front of Diamondhead. The gas line extended from the gas stations and continued down the west bound ramp. The FEMA line, for water and ice, began at the shopping center parking lot, across the I-10 and down the east bound ramp. People from several counties were arriving to line up for supplies.

About fifteen thousand Guardsmen from more than 40 states were seen about mid September in the area. (Photo by Baur)

Wally & Shirley Smith made the decision to stay in their home on Maui Place for the storm. "We will be all right," Shirley said. They had prepared their bath and vanity area with a roll-a-way, a cooler with food and drinks and lots of water in big jugs just in case the storm turned out to amount to something.

They were awakened about 5:30 a.m. on Monday by a horrendous noise. They were without TV and electricity, but they still had phone service. About 10:30 a.m., they received a call from their daughter's husband in Wisconsin; he was very concerned about them. As Shirley was talking to him, she held the phone out for him to hear the sound of the kitchen ceiling panels flopping up and down from the wind. At this time, the phone went dead.

Katrina was getting serious and Shirley began to pace the floor as she thought the world was coming to an end. The wind was a steady, gale-force wind, which would last for about 20 seconds and then slow down for a few seconds and begin again. She could hear the trees crashing around the house and the cracking of tree limbs as they broke loose and hit the ground. She reached for a cigarette, something she had given up years ago. The framed photos on the wall were fluttering. The wind seemed to continue on and on with no sign of stopping. "The wind was horrible, just a terrible noise," said Shirley.

Shirley was praying, praying that they would come out of this alive, as she knew the house could not sustain much more. She prayed for everyone that she could think of who lived in the South, as she knew they were experiencing the same wind. She gave up pacing and hunkered down in the bathroom where the noise was a little less threatening.

She kept the house dark and remained in the bathroom for the rest of the day. All this time she refused to open the blinds and look out.

Shirley, age 80 and Wally, 82, went to bed early on Monday night. The winds were still blowing and debris was still hitting the house. Shirley had still not been brave enough to look outside to see what Katrina had given them. However, they slept like a log.

Tuesday morning, Shirley opened the drapes in the back of the house to a sunny, sultry, hot summer day. As she gazed into her back yard, what she saw brought tears to her eyes. Huge trees were down everywhere, along with hundreds of broken branches and shrubs.

She walked to the front yard and tried to cross the street, which was filled with high piles of shrubs. Crawling around the debris and between houses, she reached the number three fairway on the Pine Golf Course. There she found heaps and heaps of trees covering the fairway. She attempted to walk toward the green, but found that she was blocked, so she turned around and headed for the tee box. There she was elated to find some people grilling bacon on a grill. She was totally amazed that someone was still alive in the world that Katrina had left for her.

Shirley then moved down the street among tangled wires and downed trees toward Maui Circle, where she could hear chain saws. She found men cutting up trees who agreed to cut up her downed trees and move them to the street for her. They also offered the use of their cell phone, which was working because it was an out-of-town phone. Soon she was able to leave a message for her daughter that she and Wally were safe.

For the next few days the couple had plenty to eat, as neighbors drove in from Florida, with lots of supplies. Thursday evening a neighbor invited them to a hot dog and champagne party, complete with candle light. They ate lots of peanut butter that week.

The Smiths had a battery radio and were able to hear reports from Biloxi. A "do not flush" message went out and from then on toilet waste had to buried in the back yard. "That will be a good corner to plant a shrub," Shirley replied.

Their son-in-law and daughter arrived on Saturday with tarps and tools to secure the house. The Smiths packed up and left Diamondhead for several weeks. It was a euphoric relief to leave Katrina land and Shirley could not believe how great it felt to take a shower in a motel or the pleasure of being able to flush a toilet.[18]

Friday was the scariest day of all for volunteer, Chris Marz. It was on this day that her husband told her, "We may have to pack up and leave. Things look very grim at this point."

That morning it had been announced that the grocery store was not going to be able to open. There were no grocery stores open anywhere in Hancock County. Every one had been badly damaged or destroyed. Everyone knew the "give out" trucks would not stay around forever. Where would residents purchase food once the freebees stopped? It was evident that a grocery store needed to open as soon as possible.

The first Wal-Mart to open in a tent. Waveland. (Photo by Baur)

There was still a great fear that the shootings and lootings in New Orleans could happen at Diamondhead. It was known that people were leaving there by the thousands, and Diamondhead might look appealing to some of them. No room was available to harbor more refugees. Many unknown people, who appeared to look tacky, were wandering around the area looking for food, cigarettes and drugs. Many residents became scared and wanted to leave.

However, from this point on things began to come together; supplies began to arrive and residents began to feel secure with the Alabama State Police on patrol. Every day began to look a little better. The bank opened on Friday and there was a small amount of gas trickling into the stations. One could only purchase $20 of gas at a time and with cash only. The nearest gas at this time was Tampa and $20 would not get a vehicle to reach a town where gas was available. Anyone coming into Diamondhead was asked to bring gas, the most valuable of commodities, along with gas cans, which were scarce.

What is left of a lovely Southside backyard. Swimming pool in foreground and channel behind were filled with debris.
(Photo by Baur)

On Friday afternoon, it was announced that the local grocery store employees would work around the clock during the coming weekend in an attempt to clean up and reopen the store. Some of the POA employees assisted in cleaning out the gross, smelly, rotten meat that had spoiled in the freezers.

Exactly two weeks after Katrina, the grocery store opened on September 12. It was immediately swamped with long, long lines of people. The Deli was a godsend for workers who had been eating MRE's. Six months later, the lines at the Diamondhead Market continue to be long and congested.

Over that first weekend, three special search and recover units moved into Diamondhead. All three groups had "sniffer" dogs, each trained to search for different things. The first group searched for live people among the damaged homes; the second group searched for hazardous chemicals; and the third group searched for bodies.

Survival at Diamondhead became a community effort. "The secret of survival was to pool our resources, sharing and putting everything together in one place," said Ms Collier, distribution volunteer. On Sunday, one week after the storm the food preparation and serving moved to the Methodist Church, as it had an industrial kitchen, better equipped for handling the 1,000 meals being served every day by Jeff and his staff. The food lines were long as people stood outside in the searing heat, but no one minded. Many rejoiced to find friends whom they had not heard from since the storm. There were plenty of drinks available, including coffee, juice and soft drinks.

The mission of helping refugees, both from within and outside Diamondhead, continued to grow. When the food serving shifted from the Baptist to the Methodist Church, Dr. Bill Warren, Allan Simmons, and Patricia Collier set up a warehouse and distribution center at the Baptist Church.

The distribution of basic foods took on a greater significance as Don Smith took charge and reorganized the operation. Along with many volunteers, thousands of people were served over the next three weeks. Don affectionately became known as "Don-Mart."

A few helicopters came in the next week with supplies. Soon volunteer groups from all over the nation began to arrive with food, water, clothes and medical supplies as well as shovels, hammers and tarps.

Trucks piled in with peanut butter, diapers, MRE's (Meals, Ready to Eat), water and ice. Long lines of military Humvees, ambulances, utility trucks and police cars were soon seen flooding into the region along Interstate 10 and other roads that had been opened. State Police arrived from Georgia, Florida, Alabama, Kentucky and Virginia.

At first the ice and water had to be manually unloaded, and the firemen once again helped in this capacity. Volunteers from the community helped in controlling the traffic and handing out supplies each day until the curfew forced the people off the streets at 6 p.m.

Unloading water and ice at shopping center at Diamondhead.
(Photo by Baur)

One Step at a Time

The months after Katrina was a time of waiting in line: waiting in line for ice and water, waiting for assistance at Home Depot, waiting for the insurance adjuster, waiting for FEMA to return a call and waiting in line at the grocery store.

In some areas, storm victims stood in one line to receive free ice and in a different line for water, sometimes miles apart in temperatures reaching the mid-90s.

There were lines to file insurance claims, often formed at RVs parked in lots, outside what looked like bombed-out buildings. The few reopened stores had people lining up out the doors for diapers, cleaning supplies, chain saws and lumber. It was not uncommon to wait in line for several hours to check out at a Home Depot store.

Some, after standing in line for hours, were told, "Come back tonight and we will tell you when to come back tomorrow," to stand in line again!

Warren Joseph, who moved to the Mississippi coast two years ago, has lost track of all the lines he stood in line since Katrina hit. At the Walgreen's parking lot in Gautier where they were handing out MREs and water, one person said in frustration, "Everywhere you go— you stand in a line." One woman put her hand to her sweaty forehead and moaned at the thought of getting in another line after waiting 30 minutes in line at her bank. There were few restaurants open following the storm and the line was long for people waiting for a table at a Waffle House, a restaurant known for nothing but quick service in the past.

However, those were not normal times, and everyone soon learned to be patient.

Long lines for gasoline were everywhere in coastal Louisiana and Mississippi. It was nothing to see dozens of cars bumper-to-bumper at any station that was open and had gas, as well as some that did not.

Johnnie Slater has driven a cab in Gulfport for 21 years and had never seen a gas shortage like the one shortly after the hurricane. "It has really cut back on business," he said. "The longest I stayed in line was three hours. Do you know how much time that is for a taxi driver?" As if by magic, all the lines would disappear at 6 p.m., when daily curfews kicked in. However, people would reappear shortly after the curfew lifted at 6 a.m. to begin another day of waiting.

Recovery was not happening for those who had the most damage. Trees were being removed from roofs and yards by the many tree remover people roaming the streets looking for jobs. Debris was being picked up and hauled away and small repair work was done immediately by contractors looking for work. At first it was impossible to find anyone willing to gut a house, pull out the moldy rotten wet mattresses and carpets and carry them to the curb.

Piles of household articles seen everywhere from gutting of homes.
(Photo by Gremillion)

What does gut mean? It means to clean everything out of the building down to the studs. Furniture, clothing, sheet rock, insulation, kitchen and bath cabinets, flooring, etc. had to go. In flooded homes the cupboards had to be thrown away, the floors removed and the sheet rock cut out, up to the water line, and the insulation removed. Where did this wet mess go? It was carried out to the street, which resulted in piles and piles of debris, later to be picked up by FEMA trucks. Sally Reis of Waveland said, "I'd always wanted a side-by-side refrigerator. After Katrina, I had five of them in my yard, side-by-side."

Soon crews from other states began to move into the area, stopping at houses that looked as though help was needed, offering to work for a price, sometimes too high of a price.

At first cleaning supplies were not available, especially facemasks, what everyone had to wear when they entered and worked in the flooded homes. Lots of bleach was needed to remove the terrible black and green mold, which seemed to appear overnight. Plywood was in great demand for boarding up broken windows and open walls. Chain saws, generators and shingles were also in high demand. Soon, Home Depot was flying in supplies every day, but still they could not keep up with the requests.

Backhoes began scooping up the large piles that arose in front of homes. Debris was everywhere. The cost to the U.S. Government was about $15 million to remove the debris from all of Diamondhead alone. The amount of debris from Katrina exceeded the amount of Andrew and the 9/11 New York tragedy combined.

It was difficult to travel on Diamondhead streets and county roads after the trees were pushed to the side because of the vast amount of utility trucks cutting trees, repairing lines, etc. The huge piles of debris stuck out into the street, threatening to scratch vehicles when they had to pull over for traffic.

Many cars became scratched by branches and hundreds of cars had flat tires from the multitude of nails lying all over roads and driveways.

By the following Monday, seven days after Katrina, many homes had water, with more coming on line each day. The same was true of electrical power. Each evening more lights appeared where additional homes had been "lit up."

By September 19, all homes that could have electricity restored were hooked up. This was a major accomplishment with the amount of lines lying on the ground tangled in trees branches.

South side devastation. (photo by author)

Slowly, Diamondhead evacuees began to return. Many were to find nothing left of their homes except an empty slab, or even worse than that, a water soaked house with mold covering everything. But, they hitched up their pants and were soon boarding up broken windows, arranging to have trees removed from roofs and yards and attempting to make contacts with their insurance companies, FEMA, etc. The stench from the refrigerators and freezers was unbearable and was the first job that everyone had to deal with. There was no garbage pick-up and the weather was hot, hot, hot!!!

Many, after finding their homes to be unlivable, left to live elsewhere. Before they left, they painted signs on their homes with spray paint, yes on their homes, because those walls would have to be pulled down anyway. Signs were painted on large pieces of plywood and placed in the front yard, giving the house number, (as house numbers had disappeared), and the name of their insurance company. Some signs said, *"The Shaw home. We are O.K. and at* (telephone #)." These were messages for friends and relatives letting them know that they were all right and how they could be reached. Many signs were humorous and some sad such as *"Blvd of Broken Dreams."*

It was a time for Diamondhead residents to meet their neighbors. Many residents, before Katrina, barely knew their neighbor's names; but after Katrina they were crying, laughing and treasure hunting together. People were out in their yards, as either their regular job was not functioning, the golf course was closed or the bridge game was off. (No buildings were left to play in) People listened as everyone had a story to tell, some stories so dramatic it was amazing they had survived and some thoughtful and entertaining. People soon realized how lucky they were to have a dry home and to be alive.

Everyone was attempting to make a dent in the vast amount of debris, which consisted of large branches, small twigs, pine needles, shingles, siding and many other things that had been blown in from some unknown neighbor. The sound of chain saws was everywhere from dawn to dark and high-end loaders continued to add to the continuous heaps of debris piled high on both sides of the streets.

Katrina treasures that survived the storm were found in strange and unusual places. People who lost everything in the storm were thrilled to find anything, a wedding ring or even a piece of china from a set. Wine glasses were discovered rooms away, filled with Katrina water, sitting upright. As some searched for anything left for them among the debris, here and there would be found a lovely piece of china, unbroken, sitting among the broken boards and shingles.

Roads began to fill up with FEMA trailers heading south by the thousands. With bridges and roads out, traffic in parts of the coast was down to a crawl and it took 3 to 4 times longer to get anywhere. On Interstate 10, near Diamondhead, the average daily traffic count increased from about 37,000 the same day in 2004 to 52,000 after the storm according to the DOT.

As restaurants or businesses began to open, a huge problem developed because of the lack of workers. "Hiring" signs were everywhere. There were plenty of jobs available, or at least low paying jobs, but there were few people to fill them.

Bank customers, during the first few weeks, were limited to withdrawing $200 each so there would be enough money to go around for all.

Dot and Vincent Schlafani evacuated to Florida from their home on Loulu Place on the south side of Diamondhead. When Vincent and his son arrived to check out their home, shortly after Katrina, they found the property wiped cleaned. There was not even any mud on their lot. Their boat had been left in storage, north of the area, but their neighbor's

A few precious possessions pulled from the debris (Photo by Baur)

Cabinet holding good china remains intact on wall as other cabinets had been torn from wall. (Photo by Jelinski)

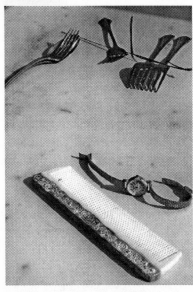

More treasures pulled from the debris. (Photo by Baur)

Child's skiis found amid destruction

45-foot boat was found high in the top of nearby trees. Those trees had to be cut down in order to remove the boat.

The Schlafani family found some of their personal effects near the airport to the west, which is about one mile from their house. They were fortunate to find a home for sale, completely furnished, on the north side of Diamondhead.[19]

Jim and Lydia Jelinski, along with their three children, Jessica 16, Jamie 13 and Joseph 11, who live on Airport Drive, south of I-10 in Diamondhead, evacuated before the storm. The children were told to take whatever they felt they would be glad to have saved when they become age 40. The family loaded up their pickup camper and left before Katrina arrived.

The house was built on piers, with the living quarters on the second and third floors. It was packed with family heirlooms. Jim, a mechanical engineer at Stennis, had built the house, with his wife Lydia 19 years ago, building it strong enough to sustain a hurricane. Four antique airplanes were left in their hangar, which sat behind and to the left of their house.

Jelinski family walking in to check their property at dusk on Tuesday morning. (Photo by Jelinski)

The family returned on Tuesday evening, the day after Katrina, walking because of the huge amount of debris with feet slipping and sliding around on the sticky mud left from the Bay of St. Louis that covered everything. They were passing house after house where only slabs remained. With each step, hopes sinking lower and lower, they neared their property. Suddenly, someone spied blue siding—up in the air—, which meant some of their house was still standing. Looking closer they found it to be still there, although heavily damaged. The house had seen four feet of water on the second floor living quarters. The debris line measured 26 and one half feet above sea level.

The wind had left someone's ladder in their yard and they placed it where the missing steps should have been and climbed into their living quarters to assess the damage.

The original steps were found two blocks away. They rescued them and replaced them to their original spot. One item found washed up into their yard was a railroad tie from the Bay of St. Louis railroad bridge; it had floated across the Bay and then two blocks north into their yard, the hardware still attached.

The Jelinski back yard as viewed from the second floor of home. Note Lydia's grand piano on ground, washed out of the house and tumbled to ground. (Photo by Jelinski)

The glass doors all across the front of the house and the rear had been washed away. Most of the appliances had floated out the empty doors and windows along with the carpets. Lydia's grand piano floated out the bay window, and was found broken into pieces, in the yard below. The porcelain doll that had been sitting on the piano was found on the ground, without a scratch on it.

Her kitchen cupboards had been wrenched from the walls and floated out of the house except one cabinet, which contained her good china. Every piece of china was intact, in place, still filled with Katrina water.

The oven was washed down the hallway and found resting in the bathroom. Everything else in the bathroom had gone out the windows except for some of their trophies and badges, which had been displayed on the wall. They were still hanging there as if nothing had ever happened.

One large heavy bathtub had been pushed through the walls, taking the studs with it and settled in another room. One double vanity ended up down below in the yard, completely intact and usable. All of the furniture was gone, but some clothing items, hanging on dinky wall hooks, were still on the wall when they entered the home. Clothes from one closet were so wrapped around the house studs that they had to be cut away to free them.

Everything in the main closet floated away, except for Lydia's wedding dress, packed on an upper shelf. The kitchen table was found three streets away, unbroken. They did find Jim's great grandmother's wooden bread-making bowl and a few other precious family heirlooms. "We feel so lucky," replied Lydia. The fish in the fish tank were never found. They had been set free to swim out to the Gulf.

Returning on Wednesday morning, poking through the debris looking for valuables, Jim found their U.S. flag and began to hang it on the house. As he was doing this a woman from the *New York Times* was looking around and asked what he was doing. He said, "I'm hanging up our flag." She said, "Why are you doing that?" "Because that's what you do." This made the couple feel better.

That same morning Jim put up a sign that said, "Open House at Jim and Lydia's."

During the next several weeks, the family removed 60 trees in their back yard, cutting them up by hand and dragging them out to the street. Debris from the condominiums several blocks to the southeast was found in their yard while their "stuff" was found to the northwest, in the woods and in other people's yards. Everything had to be carried out to the street for pickup.

Their airplane hangar was now a shell with many of the heavy steel beams bent or blown away. The four antique airplanes were all out of the hangar. Two planes were found in a ditch behind their home and a section of one was found in a neighbor's hangar. Another one was found further to the west. The planes had been tied down before they left for the storm. The hangar also housed a boat, a tractor and many other items.

The question has been raised as to why the planes were not flown out prior to the storm. Jim replied, "We had to make a decision as to leave with one truck that could carry all of the kid's belongings or take out one small plane."

A spot of blue, high in the air was the welcoming scene for the Jelinski family. The house was standing, but badly damaged. (Photo by Jelinski)

The mud left in their yard was disgustingly sticky, black and very hard to wash off. The deep ditch in the back yard was filled with wet carpet, hot water heaters, etc. It would not drain because of the debris, and soon the smell was overwhelming.

Communication flowed quite freely on the south side for the first few days after the storm as people from the north side could come and go freely. The family was receiving information about services, such as being able to take a shower at the artesian well in north Diamondhead. Once the Alabama State Troopers and National Guard arrived, no one was allowed into the area south of the highway.

A neighbor, Joann Vaz, dragged a black plastic tub to the broken off pipes of an artesian well near the Yacht Club Circle Drive area so people could have water to bath and flush their toilets.

Only water available after storm on south side of Diamondhead flowing from artesian well. (Photo by Jelinski)

Living in a friend's home in north Diamondhead, the Jelinski's were not allowed back into their property on Thursday morning. However, Friday morning at sunrise they found that the guards were not at the entrance and they were able to drive into their property. That day they moved into the third floor of the home without water, electricity, windows or doors. Lydia replies, "I wanted to redo my house anyway." The house had major damage as the secondary post supporting the building were washed away and the beams sagged down.

During the next few weeks there were many helicopters flying overhead, making them feel as though they were living in a war zone. It also looked like a war zone.

"The birds are gone; thousands of squirrels that lived in this area before Katrina were not to be seen," said Lydia. The first week after the storm one hummingbird was seen, hovering over Lydia, waiting for her to find it some food.

Clearing the debris from their yard took months. Thousands of mini blinds were hauled to the curb among everything else left in their yard from other people's homes. The family plantation bell, that previously hung in front of their home and rang every year to welcome in the New Year, was found unharmed and soon hung again on its post.

The days were very quiet and lonesome until a few homeowners began to arrive, setting up trailers to live in. The Jelinski's did not receive electricity until the middle of December.

For the Christmas season, Lydia and Jim decorated their upstairs like a department store window with Christmas lights and lighted deer, which could be seen from the street.

The Jelinskis are not quitters.[20]

Gone Forever—Our Loved Ones

One salvation to South Mississippi was that Katrina struck during daylight. Even though the day was dark from the storm, it was light enough to save some people from dying. People were able to see their way out to safety. Some were able to see objects to grab and use as shields from the relentless battering of debris flying into them.

Those caught in the surge found the water to be moving so fast and so strong that many were not able to save themselves. When the water was ten feet deep, it was probably moving as fast as 16 feet per second, which makes it even difficult to wade in. Some people will freeze from fear and allow themselves to go limp when struggling in such unrestrained waters.

Over 1,300 deaths have been confirmed, due to Katrina. There were 231 deaths in Mississippi, according to the state coroner's office, another five are still unidentified. There were 58 deaths in Hancock County. Six months after Katrina there are 300 people reported as missing in South Mississippi and 1,902 in Louisiana. Whether they are dead or just misplaced, no one knows.

Because Katrina spanned many states and because of the poor communication and wasteful efforts and resources between the states, it is difficult to determine where people are now living. Many have not notified local officials as to their new locations.

Even those dead at the time of Katrina were not spared.

Mausoleums and their contents in some cemeteries were washed away or left empty among broken tombstones. Biloxi and Gulfport have buried their dead, since the 1940s beneath large sprawling live oak trees in Southern Memorial Park Cemetery. The superintendent of the cemetery arrived as soon as the water from Katrina had receded. He discovered that Katrina had opened 131 crypts and left steel and metal caskets strewn around the beach and cemetery, dented and battered. Corpses had been lifted out of the caskets by the water and left around the beach in macabre reposes; many had been swallowed by the Gulf of Mexico, never to be found again.

He began to return bodies to the cemetery. (It was not explained as to how he accomplished this grisly task) As local people came along, many asked what they could do to help. "I just need to get these folks back," he replied to them.[21]

The morning after the storm John Bunc put on his Hancock County deputy uniform, (one that had stayed dry enough to wear) got on his bicycle and peddled toward the front of Diamondhead, planning to report for work. He found several other Hancock County officers gathered at the Ramada Inn. There were two police cars available. They divided into two groups and began rescuing people and searching for bodies. There was little communication for the first two days and requests for help came only by word of mouth. The officers worked throughout the county, wherever they were needed. Sometimes they had to go into homes by bicycle and four wheelers, as only a few homes were accessible by car. After several days a generator was set up at the dispatch office, allowing for better communication between the men. With police radios working, the men could contact the coroner's office to come and remove bodies as they were found,

During the first 5–6 days the staff at the Edmund Fahey Funeral Home in Bay St. Louis did all of the removals for Hancock County. Then the Search and Rescue teams arrived to take over the gruesome job. All of the staff members of the funeral home had evacuated their homes and sought refuge at the funeral home on Necaise Avenue. The water from Camille had not flooded that area of town and they thought themselves to be safe here. However, Katrina pushed two and one half feet of water into the building, soaking the carpets and furniture, leaving everything covered with mud, silt and sand. All the company vehicles were parked in the funeral home parking lot, and every one was flooded. This included two hearses, two town cars and two vans. The men were soon able to get the Suburban van operating for body pickups, but the other vehicles had to be replaced.

All employees, including the owner, lost their home and contents.

The staff and spouses lived at the funeral home for the next 2–3 months, sleeping on roll-a-ways. With no clothes, including suits for funerals, the directors were making funeral arrangements in t-shirts and shorts the days following Katrina.

As in New Orleans, Hancock County faced a ghastly task of collecting, identifying and then burying the corpses, many of them bloated and mangled beyond recognition. Shortly after the storm, FEMA pleaded for more body bags and refrigerated trucks for Hancock County. The coroner was threatening to place bodies in the parking lot because the county cooler was full.

On Tuesday, in Diamondhead, a rough search of homes was made by teams of firemen, but they abandoned this effort as it was futile with so much debris in homes. Later search and rescue teams from Florida and one from Cleveland searched the south side, escorted by the Diamondhead Fire Department teams. Airboats were seen searching for bodies on the Bay of St. Louis shortly after the storm.

Search and rescue teams, conducting door-to-door checks for survivors or victims, continued to tell horror stories of groups of 5–22 bodies pulled from rubble piles in some of the county's most-ravished areas. Bodies had washed up from Bay St. Louis to the shores of Diamondhead. These all turned out to be false rumors.

There were 58 fatalities in Hancock County due to Katrina. The remains of some of the dead were not released for months, even though the families were notified that there had been positive identification.

Funeral homes were inundated with reporters, demanding to know the grim and grisly details of those who had died. The directors would not divulge such material. One reporter, from USA, after much persistence, was invited to take a tour with Scott Allgood, funeral director from the Fahey Funeral Home. They parked their car north of the tracks, in Waveland, and made the walk down Coleman Avenue to the beach. Along the way, Scott continued to point out empty slabs and lots, explaining who had lived there and pointing out places of business such as Jack's Restaurant, Peterman Grocery Store and The Pier, a favorite watering hole where Scott liked to hang out. "We do not know if these people are dead or alive, but you can tell that definitely their lives will be changed if they did live through this," said Scott to the reporter. Soon there were tears running down the reporter's cheeks.

Known deaths in Diamondhead are Betty Lefler, who died of a heart attack, and Dieter and Rosie Hein, who lived and drowned at

83165 Lola Drive; all were from the Diamondhead Drive North area. The Heins had moved from Florida to escape hurricanes! It was several days before the rescue department realized that anyone had stayed in the Hein's home. They were found by a search and rescue group from Pennsylvania.

The fire department made three trips to the home of Betty Lefler before they found her. They were told that she was in her home during the storm; but with so much debris inside the house, it took three searches to find the body. She was sent back to Flint, Michigan, for burial.

For several days, armed guards stood near the front gate of the old Alcan Cable site in Bay St. Louis, where five, 53-foot, refrigerated tractor-trailers sat behind a chain-linked fence. The generators were kept running on the trucks to keep the temperature cool inside. When approached by reporters, a guard would not say what was in the trucks, instead telling them to leave the area immediately. This was a D-Mort group (Disaster Mortuary Operations Team) set up to receive bodies from this area. After several days, it was moved to Gulfport and combined with the one set up there.[22]

Evacuees Elsewhere

Conditions were not much better for those who evacuated to other cities such as Pascagoula or Baton Rouge. Life after Katrina was one big line for the 66,000 Mississippians displaced from their homes.

These people were desperate for information on their homes and the Coast as a whole. They were receiving information on TV about New Orleans but little from the Gulf Coast area and Diamondhead. The only information available was the worst possible scenario of aerial footage of the coastline. This is what they had to believe for many days.

Was anything left of their homes? Were they still standing, and/or had they been flooded with water? Pass Christian and Long Beach were mentioned as being gone! Diamondhead was never mentioned, and it was looking quite bleak for those with homes there.

On Wednesday evening a computer blog appeared on the internet with information for those interested in Diamondhead. Only those people who traveled a far enough distance to operate a working computer could get information out to the public, which was little at first; but what came out was a godsend. Residents began to receive information about certain neighborhoods. Some were very unhappy with what they were hearing, while some were relieved to hear good news.

Thanks go to Heidi Burgo, Golf Course Maintenance Administrative Assistant and POA Webmaster, who started the site on the internet and kept it going.

Hopes of returning to their homes for those sitting in motel rooms vanished, as day after day the news that reached them led them to believe that it was impossible to return to Diamondhead. Roads needed to stay open only for contractors and FEMA trucks to use. Conditions were terrible on the Coast without water and electricity. Residents were told not to come back unless they were physically able to begin removing trees from the roadways, etc.

***

*"I lost my home in the storm, but I found it! I found
it two streets away." (Unknown)*

***

When they were able to return, they came back to a nightmare—
and then more nightmares as time went on. "I'm mad, I'm sad, but just
glad to be alive," was the response from one homeowner who lost everything. Mary Beth Horn was heard to say, after plenty of tears, "I am
going to replace all of my furniture at Hudsons[23] and all of it had better
float!"

Some residents returned to their homes because they had a job
waiting for them in the area; jobs were hard to find elsewhere

Around the Area—from Paradise to Wasteland

Hurricane Katrina mangled all of South Mississippi, but most of her might—the eastern edge of the hurricane's eye—landed across the jaw of Hancock County.

Hancock County lost all of its facilities, including the jail. A temporary "pen" was set up at Kiln along with a courtroom on wheels. Most of the Hancock County facilities were located in Old Town of Bay St. Louis near the beach. The county visualized that many buildings, including several voting precincts, the courthouse, the jail, tax office and the emergency management center will have to be demolished and rebuilt. They will probably relocate farther from the water, especially since they have now obtained a stretch of county land near Hwy 603, which gives them additional possibilities.

At the first of 2006, the County was faced with a mammoth money problem as it lost 64 percent of its homes in the storm and will have an $8 million shortfall in 2006.

Katrina caused huge problems to public officials as election dates rolled around. Pass Christian lost its pollsters and all of its polling machines. Most registered voters from the Pass are now living temporarily outside of the area

The state has no law for election processes due to a natural disaster and elections must occur as in normal times.

Most schools in the area were operating out of military style Quonset huts. The Bay St. Louis-Waveland School was the last to open, on November 6, because of the late delivery of the mobile units. Teachers become excited when someone comes in with a box of pencils.

Whenever a large hurricane is approaching, it is customary for people who live off Hwy 603, north of Waveland, to drive their cars out to 603 to keep them safe from floodwaters. After Katrina, it was discovered that hundreds of these cars had received about 30 feet of water. They had been flung up, down and everywhere, and now the wind and water had left them in the ditches, most with their back ends down or up, all white from salt water and waiting for someone to come and pull them out of the ditch.

Cars in ditches along 603. Many have been removed and the road has been cleared. (Photo by Gremillion)

Six months after Katrina, about 30 per cent of the population of Hancock County has not returned. Many will not return, as there is no housing in the county available for them. There are more than 3,000 properties that owners have walked away from without signing a right of entry permit. These permits allow the Corps of Engineers to remove the smashed and falling down buildings. The county is left to sort out the mess and expense of clearing away the problems.

Hancock County recently adopted the International Building Code guidelines. Homes built in this county will be much safer and able to sustain strong winds. It also means that the county will be eligible for Community Block Grants, which will soon be available. The building codes have been voted down by supervisors for years. It took two monster hurricanes to convince them that this code needs to be enforced.

Katrina destroyed or damaged sixty percent of Mississippi's commercial shrimping fleet and ruined oyster reefs. Many fish died in rivers. It is estimated that it will take about two years for the oyster industry to begin to recover from the loss of oyster beds.

The Vietnamese Community in Biloxi and Gulfport are "boat people." Many rode out the storm on their boats, which they use to make a living; most lived in storm-ravaged neighborhoods. However, there was not one death among this group of people. Prior to the storm there were about 10,000 Vietnamese residents living on the Mississippi Coast. Those who tried to go out to shrimp shortly after the storm ruined their nets because of the massive amount of debris in the water.

Some farmers have abandoned their homesteads after losing many dairy cows in the storm. Barns and dairy sheds for 80 miles inland were shredded, and processing plants disappeared in the wind. Farmers who usually process vegetables or flowers are idle because the farmer's markets and casino restaurants are gone. Katrina wiped out about $1 billion in old-growth hardwood and pine trees, wiping out a nest egg for about 60,000 landowners.

All along the Coast, housing is an overwhelming problem. There is nothing to rent. People are now priced out of the housing market. Many low-income people are living in shabby, damaged properties. There is nowhere for them to go. Those who would like to come back to jobs that are gradually becoming available cannot find anything to rent or buy.

About the third day after Katrina, a helicopter began dropping ice and water at "The Kiln." At first supplies were thrown out of the plane, but later the planes were able to land. People would rush up, grab what they could and then retreat. Later, it became better organized, but many noticed that the greed became greater. Flood plain maps of Katrina show that the water rose the highest in the Kiln and Rotten Bayou areas.

"You cannot believe how appreciative you can be to have someone hand you some diapers, when I knew of a family who needed them so badly," said Susan Necaise.

Terre Settle lived on the north side of the Bayou, one half mile off the Kiln-Delisle Road. For 34 years, she had lived in a 120-year-old renovated schoolhouse, which sat on a high bluff. She had never seen any water come up the hill. There was a new roof on her house, hurricane shutters had recently been installed. Terre felt very secure in staying for the storm.

With hurricane shutters on the windows, the house was very dark during the storm. Terre moved around the house with a flashlight checking for roof leaks. About 11:a.m., on Monday morning, as she entered the older section of her home, she began stepping in water. The water was coming in through the doors and floor, and she noticed her small dog was swimming. She put the dog into the second story of the home, grabbed a cell phone, some bananas, a box of cookies and a bottle of water and climbed up to join the dog.

She immediately called her son in Texas and told him that water was in the house. As she was conversing with her son, the phone went dead.

Terre relates that: "Once the water had come into the house and I realized that everything was gone or ruined, I then felt as if I had nothing to worry about. All night I watched the TV set, computer and furniture banging and moving around in the water." The brackish swamp water remained in the house for eighteen hours, and it was 6:30 a.m. on Tuesday before she was able to come down.

When she was able to leave the house, she found that trees were down everywhere; and she could not move around the yard at all. She began to yell for help and a neighbor heard her calling. The two women found wire cutters and began cutting their way through fences and downed wires to get out to the road.

It took four hours to go 100 feet to the Kiln-Delisle Road. Terre was carrying her dog, which made progress even harder. The two kept losing their sense of direction and had to keep checking for the sun placement in the sky. At one point, the two women were separated from each other for one hour. "And it was so ungodly hot," said Terre.

After what seemed like an eternity, they heard the voices of men who helped them get to Diamondhead via the Kiln-Delisle Road and then double back west on I-10. The back entrance to Diamondhead was completely blocked by downed trees.

The men then returned with chain saws and tractors to begin cutting neighbors out of their property. "Our entire area had been heavily flooded with very high water. But country people take care of themselves; we did not ask for help," said Terre. [24]

From a personal perspective, the author is reminded of her association with Brett Favre. Because she is originally from Wisconsin, the following story is special to the fans of Bonita's son, Brett, who plays for the Wisconsin Green Bay Packers.

Sixteen relatives, friends, four dogs and one cat were riding out the storm at Bonita Favre's home near the Rotten Bayou, just 4 miles north of Diamondhead and 8 miles from the Gulf. This included a seven month old, a two year old, a seven year old and one 14-year-old child. As the storm began to rage early that fateful morning, Jeff suggested that they leave; but his grandmother, Meemaw, age 87, would not hear of it as she had been through the '47 hurricane, the 500-year flood and Camille in '69 and she was not going to leave this time. At midmorning, as the storm howled and trees snapped all around them, the water began to come up into the home. The water from a 40-foot storm surge, which had pushed a quarter mile into the area of Diamondhead and nearby Kiln, traveled inland up the rivers, bayous and creeks for miles; and some of this water found the Favre home. They had six feet of water in the house.

They began to place the youngsters on the kitchen counter; but as water rose even further, they moved the three younger children, the dogs and two young adults to the unfinished attic. The attic was dangerous, with very little floor area, and if one stepped off the finished area, he could plunge through the ceiling and end up in the flooded rooms below. Meemaw and Dylan, age 14, were on top of the pantry. There they remained for 6 hours.

Scott and Jeff decided to swim to a neighbor's home, a half mile away. They soon were convinced that the others would not be able to make such a swim. They returned to the home with one small boat. Jeff and his brother-in-law swam to the "party barge", but it would not start. They grabbed the life preservers. As darkness fell at the end of the day and the water subsided to about three feet deep, they fitted everyone with life preservers and moved everyone to the pool house.[25]

Since Katrina, hundreds of Wisconsin fans and organizations, who love Brett Favre with a passion, have donated money and materials to help the soaked people of the Kiln area. "They were here before the Red Cross was," replied one resident. "It is unbelievable that one person (Brett) can mean so much to a state (Wisconsin) that they take it personally to help. We expected most of our help would come from the south, but most has come from Wisconsin and other areas farther to the north of here."

Dozens of semi-trailer loads of goods have come from Wisconsin since the storm. The small town school district of Barron, Wisconsin, raised $8,000 for relief efforts in the Kiln area and a 100-person team traveled there in February to help with the rebuilding. The Brett Favre Fourward Foundation has set aside $800,000 in aid, the majority of it from Wisconsin. Twenty-two truckloads of aid, amounting to about $1 million dollars, left Green Bay for Hancock and Harrison counties. Wisconsin is like Mississippi; when it gets tough, the tough get tougher and band together.

At Jourdan River Shores in Kiln, on one square mile of land, can be found 132 FEMA trailers where homes used to be. All of the homes had been built on stilts to withstand high water from the river, but Katrina flooded every home with dirty water, leaving only mud and destruction. The homeowners live in the trailers while work is being done on their houses.

Kevin and Susan Necaise and their two children, Christopher and Lauren, rode the storm out in their home on Hilo Street. When the storm had subsided enough for them to go outside, they found trees down everywhere. They began walking down the street to check on neighbors and found many picnic benches and tables that had floated up the street from the park. People were coming out of their homes, and immediately many began to operate chain saws to help open the streets.

Susan could not make contact with her mother in Virginia or Kevin's parents in the Kiln area by phone. The next morning the family was able to work their way to Hwy 10. They had tried to go out the back entrance; but when they reached Kapalama Drive, they could go no farther.

They first went to the south side of Diamondhead to check on a friend's house. They had to walk into the area, as the roads were impassable. Slipping and sliding on the thick mat of mud that covered everything, especially the road and yards, they were able to view what remained of the house and later report to their friends.

Leaving Diamondhead they headed west on I-10 to reach the Kiln area where his parents live. The road was full of debris, and at times they had to drive on the wrong side of the road. They slowly eased their way forward, driving over electric wires that were down across the road. The road was still under water near the 603 overpass. They were very unhappy with monster trucks creating huge wakes in the water that washed over their vehicle.

*Diamondhead airport fuel tanker containing 10,000 gallons of fuel
ripped from hangar and now blocking 3 lanes of I-10.
(Photo unknown)*

The Necaises were able to reach the Kiln area, where Kevin found his family to be fine. Thirteen people lived in his parent's home for one week, keeping a generator running to keep the food from spoiling. They would operate it until the gas ran out.

His sister's home, on Bayou Cocoa Drive, had been submerged during the storm. Things were very frantic during the storm for the family as they have several small children. The parents desperately searched for items that would float when they would be forced to leave the home. They painfully discussed who would have to be left behind if they could not find enough floatable items. They never had to make the choice.

Later, "Cleaning out this home was awful," said Susan. "There were six-to-eight inches of slimy mud covering everything. You would start in one corner with a shovel and continue digging through the tons of mud." Susan even found small snakes in the mud inside the house. They had to cut up the carpet to remove it because it was so saturated with water and too heavy to move except in pieces.

"And it was so God-awful-hot!" Susan replies.

Some members of the family traveled to Waveland to acquire supplies. The first time they went, they were able to get water, ice and three MRE's for a household of 13 people. The EOC center was set up in the Save-A-Center parking lot. The windows were missing from the grocery store building, and the smell was unbelievable.

While standing in line, they watched men looting the Sears store, carrying away tools and tool chests. When the looters were reported to officers standing nearby, they were told, "Forget it, we have other things to do. The tools will rust anyway." The nearby jewelry store had also been broken into.

The Necaises helped many people, after Katrina, by opening their home to those who needed a place to stay. However, they soon discovered that some people could be very ungrateful, no matter how much was done for them. "Some did not even say 'Thank you.' Some people were also very rude while waiting in lines," said Susan.[26]

The town of Waveland, which had 6,500 people before Katrina, looks like a bomb fell on it today. "Waveland is the perfect name for this town. A wave took it away," said resident Gene Bilbo.

Every street and house from the gulf up to the railroad tracks is gone or badly damaged and has to be gutted or bulldozed away.

Devastation as far as you can see and then miles after miles of it.(Photo by unknown)

Residents who lived along the beach, and decided to stay for the storm, hunkered down on Sunday night, hoping Katrina would not be as bad as predicted. However, soon the water began to seep in through door cracks, then through the doors and windows as they began to give way. The water was soon over their ankles, then their knees and soon chest high. It was then time to head for the attic or swim out of the building. No one had time to grab shoes, glasses, medicines or valuables. The water was coming up fast and it was a *go-right-now* situation.

Those that climbed into their attics soon had water rising to the eaves. They would then attempt to chop (if they had anything to use) their way through the roof. Then they had to drop into the rolling waves with over 100 mile per hour winds beating at them. The air was full of debris flying at them, tearing away their skin and clothes. Many could not swim or endure the terrible waves and soon drowned. Many could not chop out of the roof and died there.

Some homes would begin to rock, to make terrible creaking noises, and then break up as the water moved the walls from the foundations.

Those homes closest to the beach were the first to suffer before the wind and the waves, which were strong enough to rock those homes off their foundations. As these structures would collapse, they would break apart and become floating weapons, torpedoes that would then ram and strike other buildings struggling to stay on their foundations and drive them from their pilings. A battering ram made of former buildings and powered by twenty to thirty foot waves and horrific force winds would beat against everything in its path for hours until all would come to rest in a thirty-foot high mountain of refuse and debris.

When the water retreated, hours later, there was nothing left but sticks, cars slammed against trees and thousands of trees down on roofs. After the numbers could be counted, there were only 35 homes left livable in Waveland. Whole neighborhoods had been wiped off the map, swept away, leaving behind a few bricks, a lonely set of steps to nowhere, or perhaps a marble statue or a strange looking piece of furniture that did not belong there.

On Monday morning, August 29, the Waveland Police Department members, (27 of them) decided to ride out the storm in the department headquarters, two miles from the Mississippi Sound. They felt that they would be safe there, as no storm, even Camille, had reached that far inland, or anywhere near that point. By staying there, they would be

*Unusual items found in downtown Bay St. Louis. (Photo by
Gremillion)*

available to respond to calls. The 8-foot tall glass doors had been
boarded up and the building seemed to be secure. By 7 a.m., with winds
over 120 mph, water began to lap at the building and by 8:15, when
things looked desperate, they decided to split into two groups. One half
would stay there and one half would try to make it to a nearby motel. In
that way at least some of the force would be available for rescue efforts.
Fifteen minutes later the water was 3-feet up the boarded glass door and
still rising, and rising fast. The front door was being held shut by the cur-

rent and the men could not get out. They tried another exit but it was blocked by a patrol car, which had been left parked outside. The car was lodged against the back door, which had floated in the high water.

The men were trapped in their own building, which earlier was thought to be their refuge, but later looked like doomsday.

Some of the men made a run for the attic. An agreement was made that about ten of the biggest men would begin to hurl their bodies against the front door and attempt to break through the glass and plywood. One by one, they battled the torrent of water as they fought their way out of the building.[27]

They all survived, but every one lost their personal home. Every city employee lost everything, including his or her place of work. All municipal vehicles, police cars and fire trucks were gone, swept away by the fury of Katrina.

It is estimated that 90% of Waveland's buildings were destroyed. Residents soon evacuated to live in other states except for about 100 families, who would remain to live in parking lots or in sleeping bags in their own yards. These soon gave way to tents and FEMA trailers. Buccaneer State Park became crammed with tents, which emergency and city personnel and workers called home for many months.

One man, who lives about a mile from the Waveland Inn, left his house by boat. He and his partner dragged nine people with them to higher ground.

He got to the Kmart parking lot across the street from the Holiday Inn on 5-foot seas. He unloaded his passengers on the second-floor balcony of the motel. He did not realize until the next day that there were cars in the parking lot and he had gone over the tops of them.[28]

The beautiful, new library building was completely swept away, along with thousands of books. Nothing left, but some trash. Railroad tracks had been picked up like rope and tossed over to the side in crumpled disarray. School would begin in tents, which were air-conditioned.

Nights were dark, hot, steamy and stinky with the smell of rotten animals, and the slimy mud was everywhere.

However, life did go on.

The Mayor of Waveland, Tommy Longo, sent his family to Maine to live with family. He remained in Waveland to run the city and handle the mountainous number of problems that occur after a storm of this magnitude. It was six months before the family returned to Waveland and then to live in a friend's summer home. "We are still at ground zero," said Longo six months after Katrina.

A playground for children was one of the first things rebuilt in Waveland, "so that the children would have a place to play besides in the rubble piles," replies one mother.

St. Claire's Church, on the beach, had disappeared and soon the congregation had erected a large white tent, which will serve as the church building for many years to come.

Then to add insult to injury, souvenir hunters were soon all over the city, grabbing anything that was not tied down and even those items began to disappear. One owner, whose home was reduced to rubble with only a stone fountain remaining, discovered several months later that the fountain was stolen during the night. The same thing happened to someone's boat. After the owner rescued it from a tree, loaded it onto a trailer, and left for a time, he came back and discovered that it had been towed away.

"You Loot, We Shoot!" signs were everywhere.

"Waiting on FEMA" signs were also everywhere.

Patricia Meeks of Waveland could not leave her beloved dog and potbellied pig behind. The pig had grown too large to get into the car and there were no shelters that would take pets. She died along with her pets.

Roselyn Derochers found it impossible to evacuate and care for her 17 Chihuahuas, so her decision was to stay put. She died in her Clermont Harbor home trying to rescue the dogs. Fifty people died in this area during the storm.

The Bilbo family home was in the way of the 35-foot storm surge that washed away their one-story home in Waveland. Lenora Bilbo was willed the home when she was nine years old by her grandmother. Now gone is this house that she called home for more than 40 years. The home was under five feet of water during the storm. Her husband Gene and her 13-year-old daughter Devin lost everything, even their historical photographs.

The family, along with her 87-year-old grandmother, had evacuated to Florida before the storm, but her brother remained in Waveland. While in a Dunkin' Donuts in Florida, Lenora received a phone call from her brother telling her that the water was rising very fast in the house and already up to his waist on the second floor bedroom of his house. Then the line went dead. It was four days later before Lenora received the information that he had dropped the phone in the water and had made it to the attic, which the water did not reach.

The family moved to Sierra Vista, Arizona. Her brother and mother are living in FEMA trailers. Lenore's father, who died three years ago, helped to build the post office and the American Legion Post building. These buildings along with all business and government buildings are gone. Most survived Camille but succumbed to Katrina. No photos of Lenore's father survived; water-stained, warped and faded pieces of paper remain.

Devin's schoolmates are located around the country, one in North Carolina, one in Missouri and a third in northern Mississippi. Lenora cannot bring herself to remove her home key from her keychain. "I don't want to see any more water. I cannot stand the smell of water; I want to live above sea level."[29]

Six months after Katrina very little has been done in Waveland except for debris pickup. The area is still in the demolition phase and only when this is completed can the city begin to rebuild. There is no electricity for workers to begin work and water and sewer services are just beginning to be restored. There is a FEMA trailer on about one lot per street. Few have heard from their insurance company and until the flood plans are reestablished, everyone is afraid to rebuild.

U.S. Representative, Tom Davis, from Virginia, was touring the Waveland area on the 20th of January and commented about how little had been done since his visit in September, shortly after the storm. He was frustrated with the lack of debris removal and rebuilding of homes. "We are a country that can put a man on the moon and spend hundreds of millions of dollars on the recovery of Baghdad, but we cannot get anything started here. This is a major area that needs to be rebuilt. Other house members need to visit this area to smell the stench and see the insides of some of these homes. They will then realize why the people cannot return to them. These people need help and they need it now and they are not getting it from Congress."

A little city of tents was erected after Katrina in what is called, "The Village," with 200 military style tents. The tents larger than FEMA trailers, were erected by the military and paid for by the government. The residents share rest rooms, sinks and showers, all of which are outside the tents. There the people wait for trailers or their homes to be repaired. By March 1, the number was down to 85 tents.

The new plan for Waveland will have lots of *green streets,* and the new buildings will have lots of southern-look porches and balconies.

The Hancock County Emergency Operations Center in Bay St. Louis sat 27 feet above sea level. On Sunday evening, as reports that Katrina might be worse than expected, the Center asked Diamondhead if it had a place where the Center could move its command post. The Center was told to come and look at the Diamondhead Community Center, but it decided against the move as they had a safe room in the center at Bay St. Louis. Later that evening the Red Cross and National Guard moved from the Hancock Emergency Center fearing that the building could shortly be under water.

This left about 35 city workers and police officers, the normal group was usually about 100 people, huddled together on Monday morning and watched the water rise. By mid morning, the water was three feet high inside the building. Previously the water was being blown directly from the Bay into the town.

By flashlight, the inhabitants could see no way out of their predicament and they began to panic. They decided to scrawl numbers on their arms and hands and write their names next to these numbers on paper for recovery teams to identify their bodies. However, soon the eye of the storm switched, the water began to recede and the group was safe.[30]

Scene in Bay St. Louis, just behind the Fire Dog Saloon. Notice debris pushed into the car. (Photo by author)

B ay St. Louis was a town of about 8,500 people before Katrina struck
in 2005 and known for its small town mecca of artists, shops and
beachside cafes. The "Bay" was hit hard, first by the wind and then by
the surge of 25 to 30 feet of water. The following Thursday the police
shut down the high school that had been illegally turned into a squalid,
lawless shelter, where hundreds of people were fighting and using the
floors as toilets. Hotels that withstood the storm had become refugee
camps, with victims packed into fetid rooms with no lights, water or
flushing toilets.

Casino Magic was badly damaged. Its older hotel had to be torn
down. The golf course did not reopen until December 16.

Old Town, the oldest area of Bay St. Louis, situated along the
beachfront, was a popular place for shopping and nightlife. One could
easily walk from one place to another. This area had been built along a
cliff, nearly 40 feet high in some places. The beach road was completely
gouged out along with the bluffs that the buildings sat on. Katrina swallowed all of the businesses along the water while scooping out large
pieces of land. Some buildings remain on the north side of the road, but
they are shells with nothing left inside.

About 1,000 homes were destroyed in Bay St. Louis and another
3,000 were heavily damaged by wind and water. Some buildings were
found in the middle of streets, moved from their foundations by the
water or wind. Of the 576 structures on the National Historic Register,
about 228 were completely destroyed and another 40 were barely standing.

Life was horrible during the first week and for some the hurricane meant a forced return to nature. Marilyn Garcia and William
Arnold, Jr. said they were using the woods for a bathroom. For bathing,
they rode by bicycle to a Marshy, possibly alligator-infested pond in Bay
St. Louis known as "the blue hole." Ms. Garcia stood dripping wet in her
clothes. Mr. Arnold smiled and gave a grand gesture toward the pond.
"It's artesian," he said.[31]

V ehicles left during the storm in Bay St. Louis or Waveland were
ruined when salt water poured over and submerged them. Very little help was seen for weeks in that area until private church groups from
afar began to offer their help. Homeowners would arrive now and then
to check on their property and wander through the gutted buildings,
visualizing a loved one sitting in a certain chair, sitting by a sunlit window reading or watching the Gulf of Mexico under a full moon from the

deck. Those were dreams of having lived in the home when they had been happy. Many tears were shed.

The mayor of Bay St. Louis and his wife slept for months in the local firehouse on cots. Their FEMA applications were constantly denied even though their house was completely washed away.

There was no money for most to rebuild; the insurance companies dragged their feet and would not release their decisions. Everyone was waiting for calls from someone, and this continued month after month; meanwhile these people were making mortgage payments on empty slabs. Missing payments would cause their credit to drop. Loans were given out at a snail's pace, if they were approved; most were not. Six months after Katrina, 80% of the businesses were still closed.

One couple, who had every kind of insurance that they could possibly need, collected on the flood insurance from the government, only to be told by their regular insurance company that they would receive no money for wind damage, although 15 neighbors saw their house go down before the water arrived.[32]

Gone are most of the children in the Bay, as the schools in that area were all destroyed. Families had to move to where there was a school for the children.

The "Bay" will come back along with the beachfront road. Plans are to build a retaining wall that will extend about 40 feet into the Gulf and as high as the road. Soil will be pumped into the space between the wall and the road to restore the massive chunk of land that disappeared during Katrina. The road will be widened and there will be parking along the beachfront.

Pearlington, to the west of Waveland, had 900 homes; all were flooded and at least 300 of these were completely destroyed. One 78-year-old man from the Pearlington area spent eight hours clinging to a tree. There were three people who died in that area. Six months after Katrina only 40 percent of Pearlington is cleared of debris.

Long Beach and Pass Christian were hard hit with most businesses and homes washed into debris piles or out to sea. The city of Long Beach was in the process of celebrating its 100th birthday.

The Boggsdale area in Long Beach was a community of 11 homes that belonged to the Boggs family and dated back to 1875, when Robert and Eliza Jane bought seven acres of beachfront property in the area that would later become Long Beach. Family legend claims that

Native Americans warned the couple not to build close to the Gulf. One home after another was built throughout the years, all by members of the Boggs family, and one by one they were gradually wiped out by hurricanes. In 1947 the home was built 600 feet back from the water. Eleven homes had been built on this property since Camille, but Katrina wiped all eleven off the map. "We have to start over again, but some are making their plans to rebuild. We love the water and Boggsdale is a place loved by the family," relates Claire Morrison, age 90 and matriarch of Boggsdale.[33]

Pass Christian, battered and beaten when Camille hit this area in 1969, once again received high water marks during Katrina and lost 75% of its buildings, trees, sidewalks, etc.

Many people in the Pass were trapped by the fast rising water. At least five people died on Lorraine Avenue, almost a mile from the beach, because they did not have second floors in their homes for escape. Some homes withstood the wind, but the water killed the occupants. As the surge crested over Second Street, which is very high in elevation, water covered the land to the north of the street to a height of at least 20 feet. Few who had chosen to stay were able to escape. The Pass police and rescue workers had to swim for their lives.

Mud was everywhere. Anything of value to be found had to be dug out of the mud. Homes still standing were filled with cruddy mud. Thousands of cars were found everywhere, over turned and damaged from the salt water. Nearly every home within three miles of the Gulf on Menge Avenue was flooded. Several homes were moved from their foundations and floated onto neighboring lots.

The hundreds of beautiful antebellum homes along the Hwy 90 Beachfront Drive are either gone or badly damaged. A few may be able to be rebuilt. Most will not.

Stores, motels and churches were completely eviscerated. Four months after the storm, mattresses still lie in trees. They had floated on top of the water above the tree line; and then as the water receded, they dropped between trees that were still standing or broken.

Some slabs ended up with several roofs on their property, none of them the right one. However, American flags are seen everywhere, tied to broken trees or posts or hanging among the debris piles. Slowly these flags began appearing all over, flying high and proud.

"We will not be beaten," was the attitude of many. Nevertheless, many were beaten and soon were calling moving vans to take them away from hurricanes. Robin Roberts, an anchor newsperson from ABC "Good Morning America," and a native from the Pass, has vowed to help the town rebuild.

Henderson Point in the Pass had more than 470 buildings before the storm and only about 24 were left standing but uninhabitable. Six months after Katrina torn blankets and plastic bags still dangle from treetops, mangled boats still line some of the roads and litter the woods.

FEMA trailers are now a common site, sitting on empty slabs; some residents have tried to decorate them with potted plants, fences, etc. A satellite dish balancing on a broken tree stump sits beside one trailer.

Life in a tent or FEMA trailer amidst the debris piles (Photo by Welch)

Along the entire Gulf Coast, at least 80 churches were destroyed or badly damaged during Katrina. Gone are many old historic buildings with lovely stained glass windows.

Chain saws and tree stump grinders are constant sounds; but these are hopeful people and even though "The Pass" had to rebuild in 1969, it will do it again and again, if needed. It may look a little different each time, but it will still be "The Pass."

Biloxi, (pronounced "B'lucksy"), was a lovely and slightly unknown paradise, where white sand beaches stretch for 30 miles. Prior to Katrina, one could drive along the scenic Hwy 90 and feast on the lovely old mansions, some historic and some new. Biloxi was not left untouched by Camille and definitely not by Katrina.

The storm surge of Katrina was so strong that vehicles were swept through motel windows and into lobbies. The remains of well-built homes left thousands of tons of debris more than one half mile to the north of the beach. The lovely old mansions facing the water were not spared. Very few are even "fixable." Most have been washed away or blown inland into piles of debris. Biloxi had 6,000 homes and businesses totally destroyed.

About 60 seafood-processing centers and 500 shrimp boats employing 4,300 people were wiped out, crippling an $800 million industry.

Keesler Air Force Base sustained just under one billion dollars worth of damage, causing many active positions to be transferred to other locations around the nation. Six months after the storm projects are beginning to come about under a three-year repair plan.

In 1990, the Mississippi State Legislature legalized gambling in the state but required gambling to be done on water. This was a very unwise choice; when hurricanes approached the Gulf Coast area, the casinos had to close. The state and local governments would lose nearly $500,000 in taxes each day, and 15,000 casino workers would go without a paycheck. One after another, casinos were built along the Gulf Coast, all on floating barges.

Katrina sent high water smashing through the 12 floating casinos, lifting many from the water, tearing them from their piers, and flinging them across highways, leaving only a pile of ruins. Some barges rammed into other buildings, crushing them, and some came to rest on top of motels and historic homes. Most of these huge, massive casinos built on barges were no longer where they were before the storm. The President Casino was gone. It turned up about three quarters of a mile to the west, across Hwy 90 and on land. After Katrina, 15,000-casino employees were without work and the state was taking in no revenue from them at all. The State Legislature quickly passed a bill allowing the casinos to rebuild on land.

Katrina has been called "The worst cultural disaster in U.S. History," as more than 1,000 historic structures were destroyed or badly damaged. Grasslawn, built in 1832, is now gone. Tullis-Toledano Mansion is also gone. Another historic natural landmark that has survived all storms for centuries is the spreading live oak with a unique wedding ring grown into two branches and twined into the shape of a ring. The tree is the subject of a popular Indian legend and still lives on the beach in Biloxi despite Camille or Katrina.

A former Victorian mansion. (Photo by Gremillion)

Six months after the storm, architectural students are in the Biloxi area studying these historic older buildings, such as Beauvoir, which was built in 1856. Some have survived as many as 21 hurricanes. With studs now exposed, it gives the students an opportunity to examine the quality of construction in those days. This may also reveal secrets for building hurricane proof buildings in the future.

However, the magnificent lighthouse still sits on the beach.

Along the beach in Gulfport, people are reminded of how Camille tore up the city of Gulfport, as some remnants of Camille 1969 are still visible 35 years later.

The state port of Gulfport lost 700,000 square feet of covered shed space, enough to cover more than 12 football fields. All cold storage units were wiped out.

Hundreds of semi trailers, along with huge industrial transport barges, sitting on or near the pier, were tossed like toy trucks into homes and businesses for a long distance inland. Some of these trucks had been storing chickens, pork and other perishables; and soon tons of meat began to decay in people's yards, causing a terrible stench in the hot weather. The smell was compared to sulfur and gas combined.

All businesses on the beach were a total loss. Vrazels Restaurant had a semi trailer thrown through the front window.

Hundreds of semi trailers and huge industrial transport barges were tossed like toy trucks into homes and businesses. Vrazel's Restaurant sits among the rubble. (Photo by Gremillion)

The Marine Life Facility was complexly destroyed, and the 17 dolphins left in a tank during the storm were washed out into the Mississippi Sound. After ten days all 17 were found out to sea, waiting for their trainers to find and feed them. Six of them were moved to an oceanarium in Florida. Three were housed in a pool at a local motel and then moved to the Naval Construction Battalion Center in Gulfport. The remaining four were moved to the Seabee base. Except for one who was ill, all have now found a permanent home at Atlantis, Paradise Islands in the Bahamas, where they will be cared for in a training habitat with lots of natural salt water. Their wounds from the storm have since healed

The sea lions were found, one by one, in piles of debris, under houses, in swamps 35 miles away and in back bayous. Two had to be put to death.

The entire Gulf Coast made its "come back" after gambling became legal during the '90s and the coast rose from the ashes of Hurricane Camille. Schools were improved, highways widened and motels, restaurants and shopping malls appeared everywhere. The quality of life in this area had greatly improved. South Mississippi was bursting with development and escalating its position as a national resort area in the United States. Its golf courses and white sand beaches attracted people who arrived in hoards from all over the country.

The area west of Hwy 49 and along the beach in Gulfport took the worst of the storm with all beachfront motels wiped away. Homes for miles inland in this area were damaged or destroyed. There were 3,500 homes destroyed in Gulfport, and 12,860 building and repair permits were given out during the first six months after Katrina.

Hwy 90 in Gulfport did not open to the public until December 1 in the Gulfport area and on December 17 for the Biloxi area. No street signals were in operation. Drivers could then travel from Long Beach to 1-10 in Biloxi on Hwy 90.

Fishermen attempted to stay with their boats and lost the battle. One shrimper relates how his boat was tied to five other boats during the storm. They all broke loose and continued to damage each other by banging against each other and then were pushed about four miles away from their pier. All boats were destroyed and none had insurance.

Shortly after Katrina, at the Holiday Inn in Gulfport, children and adults, some with washcloths and soap, crowded into a swimming pool that had previously been home to dolphins from a local marina.

On Thursday afternoon a temporary tenant at the Inn was seen carrying two buckets and offering to fetch water from a murky, puce-colored swimming pool to fill people's toilet tanks. In the parking lot a wharf rat the size of a small dog scurried underfoot as one person, who was living in one room with nine other family members, two dogs and a bird, unloaded bottled water from a shopping cart. After five days with no baths or showers, the children had itchy rashes on their backs, legs and stomachs, their mother said. "I'm hoping it's just from the dirty mud. It smells like death to me, all over the place."[34]

The Seabees stationed at Gulfport once again came to the rescue following the days of Katrina, as they did after Camille by making arm-to-arm sweeps through the debris looking for bodies.

At one point the Seabees were severely hampered by authorities and were not on the list of those able to cross police lines after the storm. The men were turned away when they were so desperately needed.

Shrimp boat rammed under a casino-parking ramp. One fisherman died in this boat. (Photo by Gremillion)

The storm devastated a large, large area along the Gulf Coast. Jackson County, to the east of Diamondhead, lost a lot of history. Pascagoula was 90% wet during Katrina. Slidell, Louisiana, had 10,000 homes damaged by Katrina and 4,000 destroyed.

Diamondhead Met The Challenge

"*Diamondhead dug itself out,*" *related Chip Marz.*

"*It was a thing of beauty how key people came together those first few days after the storm, to do what they did. We had no contact with anyone for days, but dazed, we continued on, not realizing we were in shock.*"

As seen in the face of most tragedies, men, women and teenagers came together in Diamondhead working together to get it back on its feet.

Diamondhead was fortunate in that many of its homes were habitable. Even though locals were left without water or electricity, most people had a place to sleep. Their cars ran, if they could find gas, and they had necessary items to use such as a hairbrush or medications. Diamondhead residents were fast to offer their services to the many that were not so fortunate.

Diamondhead opened its doors to everyone who needed help during these terrible days following Katrina. We had previously been accused of being "Rich and Republican," but the events that carried out following Katrina showed what a great group of people live here in Diamondhead. Rich and poor worked together during those trying days.

After Katrina, many people found they had nothing, but were more concerned and worried about their neighbors and friends than for themselves. Diamondhead residents were not wringing their hands and crying (they did this later), but hitched up their pants and began to work. They knew they had to try to get their lives back together in some form. They proved to be tough, hard workers and compassionate, along with their southern charm.

Residents soon became acquainted with their neighbors, as they worked to remove trees together, pooling their food, preparing it together and helping each other in many ways. Many had never spoken to each other except to say "Hi" before Katrina.

Friends and family helping the Jelinski family. (Photo by Jelinski)

In the aftermath of Katrina, the POA (Property Owners Association) and department heads of the local government made critical choices under overwhelming circumstances and did it well! They also made decisions that will affect future plans for future hurricane disaster plans.

There was never a day for weeks when there was not a positive thing happening. Immediately things were moving in the right direction toward recovery in Diamondhead.

The POA had 142 employees before the storm and 95 who are still here. These employees "busted their butts" to help get Diamondhead back in condition to live in. The first day, about one third of the crew showed up. These people were so great to come in and help out when they were suffering with their own personal losses at home.

To help Diamondhead recover, the POA assumed responsibility for many functions that it normally did not assume. It provided ten industrial dumpsters for residents to place their household trash in, since the County's contractor, Waste Management, was not able to provide regular home pickup. It placed 20 or so port-o-lets around Diamondhead to meet the needs of residents who had lost their homes and for the many contractors who arrived to help with the cleanup. It provided gas and vehicles to other emergency responders. These things were provided because they were needed to help bring Diamondhead back to some sort of normal activity.

The personnel from each department worked well together as a team with the other departments. The firemen helped the water crew with shutting off the water lines and manually shutting off the south side. "I was very impressed how everyone worked so well together to use what was available and it worked, wonderfully," said Mike Collard. "Even though we had not previously made our emergency plans."

Dumpsters for household trash were placed around Diamondhead, at various sites, at the expense of the Diamondhead POA, costing $1000 dollars a day and continued for almost a month. Portable toilets were also made available, as the sewer system was not working properly.

Three weeks after Katrina's destructive visit, our roads were clear, 98% of homes that had serviceable electrical panels had power, everyone had potable water and sewer and most had phone service. Tennis World opened that weekend and hosted a tennis social. The old 19th Hole Bar & Grill was opened for food and beverage, as the Country Club and Pro Shop were unusable. This remarkable recovery is due to the hard work and cooperation of many people and a stroke of luck. The luck is that the POA's heavy road equipment was not flooded like that of other communities closer to the Gulf. Diamondhead had the ability to literally 'dig ourselves out.'

Though battered, beaten and whipped by the worst storm in history, the people of Diamondhead remained gracious and thankful throughout the months following the storm.

There are so many heroes that have arisen from Katrina in Diamondhead that I cannot begin to mention all of them. Many of these people lost their own homes in the storm, but still continued to help out others.[35]

The First Christmas after Katrina

The month before Christmas was a "What to buy the Person who has Nothing." The boys from The Pascagoula High School Impact Show Choir recorded a song to raise funds. It was called, "Downtown Got Run Over By Katrina" and sung to the tune of "Grandma Got Run Over By a Reindeer." Santa was asked to "please be careful" when he landed on roofs, as the blue tarps were very fragile and to please check all of the tents for little children.

Spotlights were shown on huge debris piles instead of the usual homes.

Fireworks were prohibited from ringing in the New Year at all towns in Katrina Land for fear of starting fires among the debris and dead wood still to be cleared away.

Just before Christmas, the three-year-old son of a family, who had 11 feet of water in their house, believed and told everyone that "The Grinch" got his home. (One should not give this family a *Grinch Who Stole Christmas movie!*)

Piece by Piece

It took several weeks for outside help to get well organized, but by mid September, fifteen thousand Guardsmen, from more than 40 states, were to be seen around the South. The National Guard showed up at Diamondhead on the following Tuesday, one week after the storm and took over handing out the food, water and ice. Local volunteers had been doing this job for at least one week. The Guard provided help with search and rescue and support for local law enforcement agencies in all communities along the coast, including Diamondhead.

The faith-based organizations and volunteers were the lifeline for all of South Mississippi. Thousands of volunteers arrived with truck-loads of materials to help rebuild the South. Private trucks hired by church groups began to pull in and unload groceries, diapers and other staples. When they had unloaded, they were gone. They did not take time to receive thanks, etc. They remained just long enough to deliver what groups in other states had collected.

FEMA had a job that was beyond imagination and the National Guard and the Corps of Engineers soon became very efficient in the Diamondhead area. FEMA set up the blue roof program, and blue tarps began to appear on damaged roofs. The clearing of roads and debris was the largest effort that FEMA accomplished for Diamondhead. On September 13, the P.O.A announced that FEMA would be picking up debris and trash for everyone in Hancock County, but not in Diamondhead. It took a while before the agency would agree to clear private roads, (most of Diamondhead roads are private) but soon this difference of opinion was cleared. Trucks and crews, all paid for by the government through FEMA, arrived to remove the gargantuan amount of tree debris, branches, household sheetrock, cupboards, mattresses, pieces of furniture, clothing, etc. The crews were soon making a dent in this huge task, which would continue for months. They would make three passes through all the streets of Diamondhead throughout the next five months. The huge uprooted tree stumps proved to be a challenge, and many were not picked up until the following spring.

Huge uprooted trees were everywhere. (Photo by Baur)

However, many along the coast and especially in Diamondhead wondered why private companies could arrive with generators and supplies when the government or FEMA could not.

The Red Cross team arrived late, dressed in white shirts, which looked unusual, because all of the work to be done was dirty, physical work. At first, the organization appeared to be doing nothing, but they soon organized and became efficient as they handed out checks to some people who had damage from Katrina. For three days, at the Community Center, checks were processed and immediately issued in a very efficient manner. People came from Slidell, Waveland and even as far as Texas to sign up with the Red Cross at Diamondhead.

Later, this committee had to revise their policies as to who should receive checks, as they had discovered that some people were coming back three and four times for checks.

People were becoming very frustrated as it was impossible to talk with an insurance agent or a FEMA representative because there were few phones. Even after the phones were operating, most could not get through to an agent. Residents spent many hours trying to get their calls through. Some would be told that they would receive a return call, which took weeks to happen.

Many thought the insurance companies would come looking for them, but they soon found that it would be weeks and even months before an adjuster would finally make an appointment with the home-owners to discuss their losses.

It was about 9 a.m., Monday morning, when Chuck and Carol Perry noticed that water was coming in under the door of their house on Kahala Drive, near the Rotten Bayou. Bill and Rita Carlyn had joined the Perrys because they felt safer there. That part of Diamondhead had never had any water in its yards. Even when Hurricane George struck with a six-foot surge, there was no water in the yards. (The Carlyns would later discover that their home had little wind damage and no water at all)

The two men decided to go across the street to help the neighbors. By the time they crossed the street, the water was chest high.

The neighbors, Chuck and Penny Clark, their 2 children and Kim and Danny Guin and their 2 children joined the Perrys and the Carlyns at the Perry home.

The water continued to rise and it was soon decided they should go into the attic. The Clark daughter was comatose and needed to be carried. With twelve people in the large attic, they were quite comfortable, even though they had no food or water. However, they did have an ax to cut themselves out through the roof if that became necessary.

The water continued to rise very fast and it soon slammed the pull down set of stairs shut and held it tightly shut. They could see the water slapping against the soffits outside of the house through the window. Everyone was scared as they did not know how high the water would continue to rise. As the water continued to rise higher and higher, they were wondering, "Will the water stop? On the other hand, will we have to jump out of the attic? Can we get to a neighbors home? Would that house be any better than the one we are in?" The wind continued to howl, shingles blew off neighbor's roofs and all prayed that the roof above them would remain on the building.

About 3 p.m., they checked the stairwell and discovered that the water had receded. Two men dropped down, went to the front door, stepped out and found the water was still chest deep. It was receding down the street, flowing very fast, with a strong current. Knowing that they would need help to get everyone down from the attic, they started moving down the street to look for help. They met a neighbor, Norwood Landreneau, with a boat. He had jumped off his roof on Analii Street, had found the boat and managed to start the motor. He was maneuvering around the corner onto Kahala Dr. when he saw the two men.

Norwood said, "It does not move very well, don't know why." Chuck bumped into the boat and noticed why. "It's because it's still on the trailer! We have to get it off the trailer."

"We need a ride to the fire station where we hope to get help. Take us to your house and we will walk out the rest of the way. The water cannot be high all of the way to the station," said Chuck.

They continued walking down the street, against the strong current of water. They noticed a man poking his head out of a roof that he had just punched a hole through, in order to see what was happening outside. Surprised, they happened upon the fire chief, requested assistance with a backboard to get the comatose girl out of the attic, and by 6:30 p.m., everyone from the Perry home was out and safe. [36]

Later it was learned that one couple had been standing on the top of their sofa during the high water time, trying to keep their heads above the water. Fish was seen jumping among the white caps in west Diamondhead yards during the high water time. There are dozens of heroic stories from this area of Diamondhead.

One family, name unknown, who was in their attic during the storm, heard a knocking on the attic window from unknown people seeking shelter. All were later rescued.

Before the storm, some people had fled from their homes close to the Gulf to these now flooded homes, in Diamondhead, believing they were safe from high water. In some cases this placed them in a greater risk than their own homes did. After the storm, it was noticed that some Diamondhead homes on the west side had many cars in the driveway, all flooded, some filled with photo albums and valuables that had been grabbed from homes as people evacuated and fled to Diamondhead.

Hard Times Ahead

Both physical and mental health problems surfaced after Katrina. Foul air, moldy homes and stress were problems that Katrina left behind. Within weeks, people began to experience coughs, infections, rashes and broken limbs. They became jittery, tired and prone to bizarre outbursts.

Burning debris at dump areas and fumes from glue and plywood in new trailers were irritating lungs. People were falling from trees, and chain saw accidents were common.

The water that flooded tens of thousands of homes brought with it bacteria from sewage systems and dumpsters, poisons from garages and tool sheds, hazardous chemicals from businesses, and potential disease from bodies and decaying food. New soil samples taken in Mississippi show dangerous levels of pollution, including arsenic. Numerous poisons are being found in the mud and sludge left behind in yards flooded by Katrina. These poisons have remained in the soil, even though the mud has dried, and are predicted to cause illnesses for generations.

People were also having normal health problems such as Sandy Price experienced the week after the storm. She had been volunteering on the water and ice line and soon experienced pain in her abdomen. She sought help at the field hospital, which was set up in a trailer in Waveland. This trailer, which could be expanded, was manned by a crew from a relief ship sitting out in the bay. Sandy found out her appendix needed to come out. She was taken by ambulance to a Gulfport hospital, which had only opened two days before.

Stress is what hurt the residents of "Katrina Land" the most. This was termed "Post Katrina Stress Disorder." People could not sleep; they suffered and still suffer from bouts of grief, shock, mood changes, confusion, anger, marital discord, guilt and substance abuse. There are many people who still cry every day.

The Mental Health telephone lines were flooded, compared with those of pre-Katrina. People were not only becoming physically tired, but also emotionally drained. There was a greater sense of despair and loss, because the size of the storm was so large. Many were unable to make decisions or relate to others. Fights and arguments were common. In one area of the state, a brother and sister fought over a bag of ice as one shot the other.

Because the devastation is so wide spread, people cannot escape from it. Residents need to drive for miles before any sense of normalcy can be seen.

Evacuees living throughout the country are suffering recurring nightmares and drug and alcohol abuse problems. Just closing their eyes brings back memories of hanging for many hours onto a piece of wood, which was keeping them afloat, in water covered with diesel fuel or marsh grass.

In New Orleans, a second wave of death, stress, is still killing people six months later. More deaths occurred in this city during the first few months of 2006 than occurred in those same months in 2005, even though there are now fewer people.

Katrina made everything difficult; people are still bitter and searching for healing. A few are slowly offering up a smile.

We Will be Back

Businesses gradually opened in Diamondhead. The grocery store and pharmacy were needed most of all and soon opened. Ace Hardware quickly opened near the back gate of Diamondhead. Jackie O's, The Big E's and the 19th Hole were the first restaurants to open, followed by Chipotles, a new restaurant, in February.

Jon Trimmer was planning to open a restaurant in the Yacht Club building when Katrina forced him to change his plans. After searching for days in the woods and rubble for some of the hand-painted tabletops from the restaurant, Jon has now decided to open a restaurant called Pizazz in the renovated shopping center on the south side of Diamondhead.

Six months after Katrina, the first of 17 Mardi Gras parades began to roll down battered streets along the coast of Mississippi. Nothing, not even Katrina could stop the power of Mardi Gras. Floats were decorated with FEMA blue roof tarps and the loud, Carnival madness music could be heard above the cry of "Throw me something, Mister." Some have taken exception to celebrating Mardi Gras this year, but it appears to be a welcome distraction from the horrible sites still seen around, not only for the locals but also for those workers from other states.

Parade routes were shortened, there were fewer floats and fewer people lined the streets. However, some found it hard to feel in a carnival mood standing in front of cleaned off slabs or trashed buildings. Everyone was attempting to find a reason to smile.

The weekend before and on St. Paddy's Day, the locals turned out to "shake their shamrocks" as parades were held in the area, not quite as usual, but on a shortened route. The storm did not take away the local's sense of tradition or their ambition to have fun.

Let the Good Times Roll Forever in South Mississippi!

"Katrina has taught us what is really important in life and how much of life really does not matter at all." "We have discovered joy in doing the simple tasks of life and enjoying meeting new challenges," are common comments made about the daily pressures of life. "I just want to go to bed and wake up two years from now when the insurance companies are through fighting with everyone. I want to wake up to a warm and clean home that has once again risen on my slab," someone replied.

Many residents have lost their friends as they leave the coastal area due to stress or loss of homes. The heroes of the storm are those who continue to rebuild their lives and the coast without complaining. Most are too busy to complain.

The uncertainty and the stress will continue for a long time for many. People live day-by-day; the future is still too uncertain for most.

Almost 10% of Diamondhead's property has been transferred since December of 2006. There were 120 transfers in March alone. Many residents are saying, "Goodbye, Diamondhead. We loved you, but we cannot stand any more stress due to hurricanes."

Jim and Lydia Jelinski shortly after storm rehanging the family bell that disappeared during Katrina. (Photo by Jelinski)

Why Did People Stay?

During the early years of the 19th Century, people and animals in South Florida were often washed away by storm surges. Today people do not remember those storms. Diamondhead residents have been told that all land north of the Bay of St. Louis, which was soon to become Diamondhead, remained high and dry during Hurricane Camille in 1969, and all previous storms that have hit this area. Camille was known to be "the storm" which none would ever compare to. If ones property remained dry during Camille, one had nothing to worry about as far as flooding from a hurricane.

"We are tired of packing up, boarding up our houses and evacuating for places unknown, only to return and be told that we had only a few gusts of wind. Many evacuations turn out to be only a rainstorm. This storm will play itself out just like the last one. Katrina will be just another storm," was the attitude of many.

Emergency teams were out all day on the day before Katrina, driving through neighborhoods and blasting get-out-warnings from patrol loudspeakers. Mandatory evacuation means little to some people. Police cannot force people to leave their homes; they can only attempt to scare them into leaving. Police use their own way of accomplishing this by telling locals, "Write on your bodies with a permanent marker your names and social security numbers so responders can recognize your bodies when they find you dead after the storm." By nightfall on Sunday, people were still debating about whether or not to evacuate, but time was running out.

Residents who lived through the "Great Hurricane" of 1938, that struck and obliterated communities from Long Island to Providence for 1,000 miles, leaving 700 people dead and destroying entire fishing fleets, never knew what hit them. That storm, never named, occurred before the advent of hurricane tracking technology and took the country by complete surprise. However, during the summer of 2005, people had plenty of warning.

Why does the refusal to leave repeat itself storm after storm? The most common reasons that locals give for staying are as follows:

a. Not taking it seriously—it will strike elsewhere!
b. A fear of looters ransacking their homes if they leave
c. They might be able to save items or their home if they stay
d. A lack of shelters that will take pets, who are a part of the family and cannot be left behind
e. Bad experiences in evacuating for previous storms
f. Too hard, too expensive and too much stress for older people, especially if they use oxygen or wheel chairs
g. Many refuse to leave a relative, a neighbor or pets no matter how fearful they are of the storm
h. There are always a few who stick around for the "entertainment."

Some feel that experiencing a mighty hurricane will be an exciting feat to behold. To see the salt water spraying high along the coast, ahead of the storm, is an exhilarating experience. Many live to boastfully tell of the experience, but many have discovered that this is utter foolery.

For centuries, local families have kept the tradition of gathering with family or friends in the comfort of someone's home, a location that had always been safe during previous hurricanes. As at a family reunion, people carry their valuables along with food, drink and candles and look forward to a day or night of family fun. With the radios squawking, giving the latest condition of the present storm as it moves closer to shore, people tell stories of past hurricanes while kids run around and telephone calls are made to other relatives and friends.

Dr. Louis and Harneitha Maxey, of Long Beach, ages 92 and 75, were just plain tired of evacuating. The health of Louis had suffered each time they evacuated, so this time they made the decision to stay in their home. Both perished in the storm, as did many who made the same choice.[37]

People have a powerful attraction to the water and will continue to rebuild near water time and again. This is where tourists go for vacations. The magnetism of the beauty of the beaches pulls people back even when danger lurks. "It's because of the water. We love the water," one resident replied.

However, most people who "stuck it out" for Katrina have since stated that they will never do it again. Al Revel, storm survivor remarks, "Next storm, I am going to leave!" Diamondhead will probably be a ghost town when the next Hurricane Category 5 is coming toward it.

Betsey & Dick Nolan's 35 year old home on Maunalani Place near the Rotten Bayou in north Diamondhead was lifted from its foundations, floated out to the street and then down the street where it came to rest upon a main water line, one half in the street and one half on someone's property. It had to be demolished. Their neighbor's homes were all flooded with 10 to 12 feet of water.

After evacuating for Katrina Lady and Bob Bruce returned to find their home had been under water up into the attic even though the house was up on pilings. The Rotten Bayou is right behind their property. They had moved items to higher places expecting some water if the storm should hit this area, but nothing like this. The entire neighborhood stuck together, helping each other to heal the wounds.

Why Build on a Beach?

The story of Hurricane Katrina began more than three centuries ago when European immigrants, unlike the American Indians, began to build settlements on storm-vulnerable coasts.

Before humans began to inhabit this area, common floods would deposit silt over the floodplains, replacing the land that had eroded. With the Mississippi River contained between dikes, this natural renewal has been halted and 85 million tons of waterborne silt is being forced over the edge of the continental shelf each year, where instead of rejuvenating the land, the sediment tumbles into the depths of the Gulf of Mexico. Pumping water and gas from the ground also aggravates the situation.

The site chosen for New Orleans had many advantages. Louisiana Indians had long used the area as a depot and market for goods carried between the two waterways. The site was chosen because it was the shortest distance between the Mississippi River and Lake Pontchartrain. The narrow strip of land also aided rapid troop movements, and the river's curve slowed enemy ships approaching from downriver. This looked to be a wonderful spot for a city.

Hundreds of years ago, the residents of New Orleans learned how to build levees to hold the Gulf water back from the land. However, sometimes, as in Katrina, the water is stronger than any man made object. Many buildings were damaged by the winds of Katrina, but the greatest damage occurred when it was thought that the city had escaped from the storm. The levees began to give way and much of the city became submerged under as much as 15 feet of water, causing great mayhem in the big city. They were definitely not ready for Katrina. Many people were trapped in their attics and were later found drowned.

Sections of New Orleans have sunk to nearly ten feet below sea level. To the south of the city, as low-lying lands have disappeared under the water, the Gulf has been creeping closer and closer.

Why do people continue to live there? People will always figure out how to live and thrive anywhere. Meanwhile, New Orleans is slowly sinking.

Many people are asked, "Why stay near the beach, go further inland." One local, a fisherman, replied to that statement, "I'm a salt-water man; I don't want to go to the country." Another said, "I love the water and here I stay."

The Good and the Bad

Catastrophes bring out the worst and best in people, and The Gulf Coast saw both following Katrina. The old saying; "Someone is getting rich off of misery," also pertained to Katrina. There were those who took advantage of those in need, especially the elderly, by various methods of fraud and looting increased the misery.

One elderly woman in Diamondhead paid a transient tree company $18,000 to remove trees from her roof and yard before she realized that this was way out of line for this amount of work. She had no one to discuss the problem with, and the company had warned her that her house would be damaged unless she had the work done immediately.

Then there were the thousands who came from afar, giving up wages, working tirelessly to help a fellow man in trouble.

The support from individuals, countless civic and faith-based groups, schools, churches, corporations, military and others has been overwhelming. Volunteers such as those associated with the Campus Crusade for Christ in the Pass, who had gutted 600 homes in six months, also hung sheet rock, painted and tackled other necessary jobs.

Thousands of volunteer college students descended on the South during their spring break in 2006 to assist in pulling carpet and sheet rock from devastated buildings. Seven hundred law students from Jackson to Belgium opted to forego their traditional spring break to spend one week on the coast. Instead of pulling moldy sheetrock from broken homes, they provided free law advice to those who needed it.

The Mennonites and the Amish arrived, working diligently and quietly, never complaining and never seeking publicity. They continue to return to the Coast with truckloads of building supplies and furniture.

Caravans of utility trucks, ambulances, police, firefighters and emergency personnel were soon pouring into the area of South Mississippi.

Volunteers from Montclair, Virginia, arrived in Diamondhead around the end of February to help rebuild homes destroyed by Katrina. This group, called Mend-A-House, is coordinated by Jay Todd, the father of Michelle Dunn who lost her home on Amoka Drive. Michelle and Peter Dunn had six and one half feet of water in their home. Todd became interested in helping and getting involved in the Diamondhead area and has since rounded up a team of volunteers to help rebuild some of Diamondhead's trashed homes. The volunteers stay at the Baptist Church, which accommodates groups from around the country who continue to arrive to help rebuild this area. Todd has made the 16 hour drive several times since Katrina to help with the project. Mend-a-House unloaded a tractor-trailer full of appliances, all donated for this area. The truck held refrigerators, washers, dryers, dishwashers and other large appliances all donated from the Montclair area, some used, some new.[38]

Volunteers needed housing and food during the time they were here to work, a huge problem when there was little housing for any one on the Coast. Churches and tent cities helped in this capacity. Volunteers will be needed to help the Coast for many years to come as Mississippi had close to 170,000 homes destroyed according to the Red Cross.

Three divisions of EPA emergency response teams of 60 people have been rotating two-week tours in South Mississippi, collecting or gathering amongst the debris hazardous materials, such as bottles of ammonia and large fuel tanks. All are volunteers and some have done a two-week tour three different times. They come from all over the U.S. Six months after Katrina, they have collected over 200,000 units and 800 aboveground storage tanks in Hancock County alone. They also have contained and treated about 39,000 gallons of spilled fuel. The collection point is set up on Stennis Space Center property, where piles of rusted and cracked propane canisters can be seen. Propane tanks float on top of the water and thousands have been found, mostly in wooded areas and among the debris.

Within 72 hours after Hurricane Katrina struck, the Utah based, charitable Morrell Foundation's iCare Quick Response Team visited South Mississippi and assessed how they could best serve the victims of America's worst natural disaster. Morrell Foundation President, Merrill Osmond, of the famed Osmond Family entertainment dynasty, has put his life on hold to help the people of South Mississippi.

Morrell provides temporary housing and employment for relief workers and survivors. The company opened the first of four iCare Village complexes on October 12 in Buccaneer State Park in Waveland. Built on land donated by the State of Mississippi, the village's 10,000 square foot base unit came together remarkably fast, with the main structure erected in just three days. On top of providing accommodations for 300 people, the site maintains a medical clinic and dining and laundry facilities. It had electricity, water, sewer and air conditioning. It had 44 rooms, 15 toilets and showers and a computer lab. It was the volunteer headquarters and community center for the area and served as a support center.

The FEMA plan uses thousands of volunteers but does not provide any housing for them. This group provided housing that was needed. The iCare Village will be shut down for the 2006 hurricane season as the company feels that it is located too near to the water. Wood frame houses are now being built in the back of the park. This relief center has housed thousands of volunteers helping with recovery efforts.[39]

Late Monday afternoon, the day of the storm, someone at the country club spotted a family of seven people struggling across the driving range on foot. It was the Dye family from the east side of Diamondhead. Some did not even have shoes! Their home on Alkii Way had collapsed under the high water pushed in from the Bay of St. Louis and they walked or swam out with just the clothes on their backs. "We took them in, gave them some dry clothes and shoes as well as food and drink. Their survival stories were hard to believe. Diamondhead, north of the interstate had been hit by the storm surge! High water had pushed into the city by the high storm surge that hit on the Gulf beaches to the south of us," related Chip Marz.

The family of Bill Dye, his sons, Richard, age 15 and Michael, age 19 and Bill's brother, Curtis and wife Cheri, braced for Katrina. They were well prepared for this storm with 60 gallons of gasoline in the garage, a large generator, enough water and food for a week and windows that were boarded up.

Bill's house was on Alki Way, just north of the Interstate. Everyone knew that houses north of I-10, were safe, so the family was not worried about anything. They were set!

Bill was employed by Sears in Waveland and worked all day Saturday and went to work on Sunday because they had just received a big shipment of generators. Generators are a huge sale item just before hurricanes are predicted to arrive.

Bill woke up early Monday morning and the wind was blowing hard. Bill loves storms and prefers rain to sunshine. He was sitting on his enclosed front porch watching tree limbs blowing from trees and debris blowing over the top of the house.

About 9:30 a.m., the front yard was filled with water, but this was not uncommon during heavy rainstorms. In the 27 years since the house had been built, there had never been any water in the house. The ditch was filling up in front of the house, but Bill felt confident that the water would never go over the interstate, which was built high.

When the water kept rising, Bill began to smell kerosene. Looking closely at the water, he noticed it had color sheen on it. The odor was strong and becoming stronger and stronger. He learned later that it was gas from the marina gas tanks, which were across the Interstate and near the Bay.

"Hey Dad," said one his sons, "There is water coming in under the front door and running into the great room." They began to pick items up off the floor, placing them on beds, etc.

The water kept rising and was coming in through the door and window frames. There was no current and no splashing or wave like activity. Bill went into the bedroom and the water was up to his ankles. "This cannot be. Water will never come into my house."

Bill looked out the window; he could see the front door and saw that the water was up to the doorknob. The house was trying to keep the water out, but not succeeding very well. "We are now in serious trouble and we have to think fast and clear, or we are going to get hurt or even killed," said Bill to his brother.

Then one son said, "Dad, this water is salty." Terror set in as they realized that this water was not running down to them from the golf course; it was coming in from the Bay of St. Louis and out of the Gulf of Mexico. Later his son would tell him that he had opened the back door, which faces the interstate. The entire back yard was under water, the interstate was under water and the water had white caps on it. He just closed the door and told no one.

"We have to get out of here and fast. Grab what you need to take; it is now survival time; forget the photos, etc," yelled Bill. He grabbed a raincoat, turned around and noticed that the furniture was floating and had him trapped in the room. He tried to push the dresser out of the way, which did not work, then he tried to dive under it. As he did, he moved it enough to get past the heavy furniture and leave the room.

Someone said, "Hey Dad, the wall just collapsed between the

kitchen and the garage and everything from the garage is floating into the house." The sheetrock had washed away and only the wall studs were left. The gasoline tanks had upended and gasoline was spilling into the water, which was running into the house. The cars were floating in the garage. The refrigerator had tipped over and was floating around the kitchen.

Bill grabbed the handle of the front door to let everyone out. The door was violently pushed inward by the higher water outside the building. The water was about two feet deeper outside the house than inside. Water began rushing in around Bill, but he managed to keep his balance.

At this point, they all felt that they were going to die. It was time to try to save their lives.

They waded out to the driveway where a pickup truck belonging to Curtis was parked. The water was about five feet high and Richard jumped onto the roof of the pickup. The truck began to float and Bill knew that this was not going to be the solution to their problem.

High water in Waveland. Taken during the storm. (Photo by Condon)

They decided to walk out to the street, turn left and swim or walk toward Diamondhead Drive East. If they could make it to the golf course, they would be on much higher ground than they presently were. Bill would go first; and if he did not make it, they should climb onto the roof of the house.

Everything worked fine and he signaled for the rest to follow him. This was about 10:15 or 10:30 a.m., at the height of the storm. There were trees down all over and they had to climb over several large trees to gain headway. Curtis and Cheri were each carrying a small dog. Everyone was frightened of what might be in the water, snakes, wild pigs, even perhaps an alligator. Power lines were down all over and so they were worried about another tree falling on them. The trees were twisting in horrible, freakish contortions and were falling all around.

With water only up to their waists they found a home with a dry yard. The porch was protection from the winds and rain. The water began to creep up into the yard and up the side of the house. After about 15 minutes, that began to look like a poor place to stay.

They left that porch and entered the street, which had been dry 15 minutes before and was now chest high in water. They continued up the street and found another dry street and porch, which lasted another 15 minutes, but the water was still rising. They continued on towards Diamondhead Drive East. While they were walking, they could not hear her at the time because of the winds, but a woman down the street, clinging to a tree, was screaming for help.

They found protection on a porch, three homes to the east, on the south side of the street.

They spotted a big, 300-pound pig, swimming toward them. They were afraid that it would want their place, but it swam on by. The water was about three feet deep on Diamondhead Drive. Roofs were blowing off houses all around them. They could feel the walls of the house next to them pulsating, and the windows were shaking and moving in and out. The garage door was blowing in and out and threatening to blow away.

Richard was now freezing and Bill wrapped him in the raincoat that he had grabbed before leaving the house. The party discussed breaking into the house for shelter and the possibility of being arrested, if they did so. Was it justifiable to break into a house when in need of protection from the elements in order to save their lives? However, this was to be a last resort effort.

Bill began watching the water slowly continue to rise on the bricks of the house to the west. After about 15 minutes of watching, the water stopped and then for about 10–12 minutes, it stayed at that position and then slowly began to recede.

All morning the wind had been blowing from the southeast. On the east side of Diamondhead there never was calm in the storm or reversal in wind direction. The eye had passed to the west of Diamondhead.

The family had been on the porch for about 2 1/2 to 3 hours. Richard was still chilled and in shock. Bill walked over to a car sitting in the driveway and found it to be unlocked. Richard was moved to this vehicle where he immediately began to warm up.

Bill decided to walk back to his house and see what could be salvaged. The water was completely gone and he was crawling over, and in some places, under the trees. Power lines were down and messed in with the branches.

Party dresses swinging in the breeze on hangars in destroyed eastside Diamondhead home. (Photo by Baur)

He came to a house on the west side of the street just before the turn and noticed that the windows had literally blown out. The window frames were lying in the yard and the curtains were blowing to the outside. It appeared as though the house had filled up with water; and when the outside water receded, the inside water was still being held in by the walls, which soon could not stand the pressure and collapsed outward. The items and furniture from the house had poured out of the house with the water and settled across the street. The yard held a large dead dog, left there by the receding waters.

Bill kept walking, made the turn and could see that the roof of his house was flat on the ground. There were still about 2–3 feet of water in his yard. Everywhere he looked; there were splintered boards and piles of utility lines. He decided there was no use to venture any further. He walked back to the family and told them what he had found. About 4:30 p.m., they began to walk towards the Country Club, where Bill knew the security force was stationed. The wind was still blowing about 40 miles per hour.

Someone with a pick up truck attempted to take them to the clubhouse, but he could not get through the streets because of the downed trees. They left the truck and continued crawling around trees until they reached the clubhouse. The building was missing some of its roof and the inside was very wet. They found everyone there eating steaks, as there was no way to keep the meat in the freezers from spoiling. Everyone at the clubhouse had a great steak supper on Monday night.

When it turned dark that night, it became very dark and very scary. Candles were placed on the tables. Someone arrived and declared that the building was unsafe to be in. Unable to find any place better, the Dye family ignored the warning and settled down in a hallway to spend the night sleeping on the floor, along with the security force and some members of the board of directors. Everyone soon learned the meaning of dark as no candles were allowed after they settled down to sleep.

The next morning everyone was ordered out of the building. The two security cars sitting in the front circle, with eight flat tires, were going nowhere. A POA truck arrived and informed them that residents had come out of their homes and cleared a path down to the gas station area and that the Baptist Church was taking in refugees. They climbed into this truck and made a weird trip around and under tree branches, some not clearing the truck top.

The Dye family was fortunate in that no one had been hurt, except for being very wet and frightened. Both Curtis and Bill lost their homes. Bill had been wearing the same pair of wet shoes for 48 hours before taking them off. As he removed his socks he found that there was no skin left on the top of his toes.

It was 4–5 days before Bill was able to get back to his house and check the damage. He had left the house without his billfold, which held his driver's license, etc. Weeks later, searching through the debris, four blocks to the west, he spotted his bedroom dresser. In the drawer, he found his billfold along with his driver's license and other personal information. All of his sentimental items were lost, such as photos and things that his mother had left him, etc.

His house had slid away from the foundation and settled to the side. Nothing could be salvaged because of the water, which had reached above the ceilings, and also because of the diesel fuel that had spilled into it. The house had filled up with water; and with the windows boarded up, the water could not immediately flow out of the house. When the outside water receded, the walls exploded with the bricks spilling to the outside. All four walls went out. Engineers believe that the roof stayed, but the water ripped the house from the slab and slid it to the side and the studs went with the roof pulling it from the foundation. His garage was in the street. Most of the appliances, sofas, etc. were still in the yard.

Bill says, "I was luckier than those over on the west side, as the storm cleaned my lot off for me. I only had to bulldoze the mess away and start from scratch. I did not have to strip sheetrock, tear out the icky black moldy carpeting and clean the mold off the two by fours."

The Dyes remained at the Baptist Church for several days before moving to his nephew's mobile home in Holiday Village in the northeast section of Diamondhead. That trailer was not even damaged.

Someone offered Bill the use of a minivan for a time as he had no car. "The generosity of people has been just incredible," said Bill. "Loaning me a car made my day. I have never been without transportation and I was tired of begging rides."

Shortly after this, Bill was offered a job with local security as his job with Sears in Waveland was gone.[40]

Items I Remember by Dr. Patricia Collier

Week One:

- The unbearable heat—in the high 90s with high humidity, making the heat index in the 110s.
- Teenagers keeping an eye on the children, freeing up their parents for volunteer work.
- Hearing stories of people being beaten and robbed at the Ramada Inn.
- National Guardsmen standing guard at the grocery store.
- I.D.s being checked at the front gate to allow only Diamondhead residents in; however, the back gate was wide open for looters.
- Brandon Cole nearly catching someone trying to enter his house on Pokai Court, they fled in a dark pickup.
- A ladder stolen from a neighbors home, only 2 houses down from me.

Week Two:

- The Wiggins Wal-Mart letting in only a few people at a time, because of shoplifting.
- Angry people when supplies became low.
- The truckloads of supplies coming in from all over the country, more clothes than we could ever need were piled in the old sanctuary.
- The busy signal of the Red Cross number.

- The busy signal of the FEMA number.

Week Three:

- The sight of Bill Dye's house smashed to the ground.
- My first sight of the Waveland Wal-Mart and the large gaping center entrance.
- Tours of the destruction to volunteers.
- Helping clean someone's home. There was so much mud and the stench was awful! I spilled dirty bleach water all over me.
- Marines unloading a truckload of supplies in a matter of minutes.
- The thrill of seeing soap and toilet paper while unloading supplies.
- Seeing volunteers from the San Francisco Fire Department on Main Street in Bay St. Louis; this California girl was mighty proud to see them.
- The sight of Amanda Love's grand piano in pieces in the street.
- The blue house (Nolan) in the middle of Maunalani Pl., which had floated off its foundation and down the street.
- Flashbacks to Katrina during Rita because of sight and sound recollection.
- Our grocery store re-opening.
- Wal-Mart in Waveland operating from a circus tent for three weeks—then to a larger tent.
- Limited menu at McDonalds—offering canned Cokes

Week Four:

- Cleaning Ann Dye's house after four men stayed there after the storm.
- My first trip down Nicholson and Coleman to the Beach in Waveland.
- The stairs that lead to nowhere in Bay St. Louis.
- The RR tracks in Waveland looking fine to the east, but like a roller coaster to the west, and a house on top of the tracks.
- Seeing the geese return and hearing my first songbird.
- Seeing a large raccoon near the fire station, a large armadillo in my yard on 10/2, discovering my cats are killing rats—not mice—rats!

Maisie Condon tried to evacuate with her dog, Shelley. She lived near the corner of Waveland Avenue and Hwy 90 in Waveland. After gassing and loading her car, she locked her door and discovered her vehicle would not start. It had been drained of gas. There was no gas available anywhere in Waveland, so, she unloaded her items and hunkered down in her apartment and waited for Katrina to pass over. When her roof blew off, she grabbed the mattress off her bed, dragged it into the bathroom and covered herself and Shelley. The storm let up slightly and she went out onto the balcony and took some photos of the high water, which was now nearing the roofs of the Mexican Restaurant and Hudson's Discount Center across the street. Her car had floated away. The water continued to rise and she was now sitting in water in her second floor apartment with no roof over her head.

Maisie lived here for ten days before she was able to find someone to take her in. During this time, she rescued a large dog, which was still attached to a chain. His paws were torn and bleeding. She was only grateful to be alive and has since moved north.

Six months later

Many areas in South Mississippi look the same as they did on day one after Katrina and as if time has stood still for the past six months. Visitors and workers arriving from the North are shocked to see the devastation that looks as if the storm hit yesterday. After 180 days of work and frustration, more than 10,000 Mississippians remain homeless with some still living in tents, even though temperatures often plunged into the low 30's and 20's. People are still sleeping in cars or living with relatives. Debris still remains to be hauled away. In some areas, unemployment is comparable to that of the Great Depression.

People along the coast are waiting, waiting on the government to decide how high they need to build their next home, waiting for the insurance companies to decide if they will receive any funds at all. Some are waiting on carpenters, who are very few in number, and everyone is waiting for windows and doors to come from the manufacturers. When they do come in, after months of waiting, they arrive broken and must be reordered. Everyone has learned to have patience.

Signs on devastated properties are slowly being changed from *Blvd of Broken Dreams* to *Hwy of Hope*.

Slowly, but surely, the signs of progress are beginning to show. Some areas along the coast are showing no progress at all, still looking as though a bomb was dropped on them. Many homes are now being removed by heavy equipment, leaving only the slab.

***

"Oh my, this will take weeks to clean up."
(Chip Marz)
***

Two-year-old children are still living in tents or trailers that do not have decent facilities. Some people are still living in cars. A 240-square-foot FEMA trailer, sitting amid the rubble of empty slabs or collapsed homes, is where many survivors deal with day-to-day hassles. The propane tank may be empty, which means a cold shower, but most are hopeful. In the Pass, under a tent on Hwy 90, over 1,500 meals are still being served each day. Many streets along the Gulf are still without water and sewer. Some people are living on their second floor while they are rebuilding their first floor living quarters. "We have walls now," is one happy response.

The coastal towns are by no means back to normal and will not be for years. Not all towns are recovering at the same rate. Waveland, Bay St. Louis and Pass Christian that were almost totally swept away are recovering much slower than Diamondhead. Recovery is also uneven for individuals, as some are back in their homes, while many are still waiting for a job, for insurance money or sheet rock. One cannot imagine the smiles on faces when a load of sheet rock finally arrives.

The lovely white sand beach, the water of the Gulf of Mexico that extends for miles, riverbeds and residential channels are still littered with debris. Much of the sand has been sifted and cleaned with a machine that removes debris, but the water is filled with stationary trash, such as air conditioners, appliances, tree branches and pieces of torn metal roofs. These items are lying in wait for the careless boater. There are probably more than 3 million cubic yards of debris to be removed from the water in the three Mississippi counties that were affected by Katrina. The water will eventually be cleaned for at least four miles out into the Gulf of Mexico.

Some volunteer groups, such as the Seabees were seen using large construction equipment to remove the large pieces of sofas, pieces of carpet and clothes still attached to their hangars. They work during low tide; the job is monumental and will go on for some time. Relief workers continue to stream into South Mississippi.

Within 60 days of the storm, Mississippi had received 16,000 FEMA trailers. Every open field became a temporary trailer park, where the trailers sat waiting for families. Many chose to have the trailer set up on their destroyed property or on their driveways, but first water and sewer had to be hooked up on the site. In some places, there was no chance of getting utilities hooked up on an owner's lot.

FEMA had delivered 36,700 trailers in Mississippi by the end of February, but still people were in need of housing. Hancock County

Biloxi beaches after the storm. (Photo by Gremillion)

received 8,553 trailers, but 700 hundred families in the county were still awaiting trailers. Many have given up on the government and have purchased their own trailers. There are more than 100,000 people living in trailers in Mississippi. They have become known as the "Katrina tin condos." Most of the area near the Gulf is virtually trailer parks with an occasional building being worked on. These flimsy travel trailers, not sturdy enough to withstand a strong southern thunderstorm, are already worrying the authorities with the upcoming hurricane season only months away. They may become flying missiles and dangerous projectiles.

FEMA has given out $160 million to individuals in Hancock County alone, and still many people are living among the trash of their precious homes. Katrina left more than 40 million cubic yards of debris to be cleared and hauled away.

Bechtell Corporation of San Francisco was offered a $100 million no-bid contract in August to distribute the trailers to the needy, hook them up and maintain them. Hundreds of the FEMA trailers were soon breaking down; waters heaters were failing; doors and locks jammed easily; the appliances were inferior and failed to work; and electrical systems went kaput. These trailers had been manufactured in machine-gun fashion and construction was shoddy.

Senator Joe Lieberman, from Connecticut, said, "…the government failed its test. I am disappointed that I do not see more progress four months after Katrina. People in Mississippi have to deal with too much bureaucracy and too much red tape."

There have been 220,990 Katrina insurance claims filed in Mississippi since Katrina and by March 1, 2006, the companies had paid out $5.9 billion. Most of this was for wind damage. Flood damage is still being negotiated for most policyholders.

Property owners are learning the meaning of what the insurance companies consider flooding, as water coming from above or sky down. Water coming from the ground up is referred to as inundation. Now will begin the court battles as to who will pay, the owner or the insurance companies. There are reports of insurance companies asking engineers to alter their reports or the company will hire a new engineer. The companies are claiming to have settled 94 per cent of the claims, but property owners are having a hard time believing that figure. Flood victims have now become flood policy victims.

There were 35,000 homeowners in Mississippi who did not have flood insurance, only because they had been told by the national government that they were not located in a flood prone area. Only after Katrina struck did Mississippi Insurance Commissioner, George Dale, realize that flood insurance rate maps were very inaccurate. Most flooded properties in Diamondhead were designated to be outside the flood area on the 1980's maps. New maps were being updated when Katrina struck. Most people who lived in a flood plain area did have flood insurance. The fact that the flood plain maps were outdated was due to a process that moved too slowly and the homeowners are now having to pay for it.

This has been little reassurance for many hundreds of homeowners caught with no flood insurance when water rose to nearly 12 feet in their homes. Thousands remain without claim checks and no way to begin rebuilding. Senator Trent Lott emphasized, "The insurance industry has done an absolutely abysmal job in responding to their south Mississippi policy holders."

The Corps of Engineers provided an unknown amount of manual hours and thousands of truckloads of debris removal. The Red Cross spent $185 million in South Mississippi alone.

While visiting the Katrina devastation, shortly after the disaster,

President Bush promised that the country would "restore and make it right." However, help in the first three months was only to provide food, shelter and other needed necessities. Little help has come forth for restoration.

When residents applied for the personal low interest loans promised to them by the government, many were rejected. After 100 days and 276,000 loan applications, 82 percent of the one third that had been reviewed, had been rejected.

Of the 7,000 small business loans applied for over the State of Mississippi at the end of 2005, only about 400 had been approved. Those who had been approved were still waiting for their money. However, at the six-month anniversary, the administration announced that it had received more than 380,000 requests and approved $5.4 billion in loans to 76,000 applicants throughout the South.

Flying out of Gulfport at Christmas, the author could see many, many homes with blue tarps still dotting the landscape. It looked as thought one-half of homes left standing after Katrina, were still without roofs.

"My Blue roof blew off," was being heard around the area. Six months later, there are still many blue roofs to be seen, and other problems arise daily. Shopping is a labor, with long lines and long waits for ordered materials. The few stores now open have reduced hours due to scarce labor. All motels and condos, that have available rooms, are rented by workers and not available to the general public.

Property lines are almost impossible to re-establish as markers were wiped out in the hardest hit areas. Crews search for buried pipes, fence lines and anything that will establish a lot line.

Local schools are meeting the challenge of having to lay off teachers and administrators because the number of students has declined, due to their having no homes to live in around the area. With such a low tax base, it will be difficult for schools to continue to meet their payrolls for the next few years. The losses to school districts in Mississippi by Katrina total nearly $700 million. Things look very grim for those districts near the water.

Postal services were badly interrupted when nine post offices were lost to the storm, although employees remained stable. The U.S. Postal Service is wondering where the people will resettle and where postal services will be needed the most. Areas such as Pearlington and Waveland are being closely watched.

Diamondhead is beginning to look pre-Katrina along Golf Club

Drive and other streets that were not hit hard by the storm; however, the flooded areas are only beginning to come together. One can recognize which homes were flooded as doors and windows have been removed, making the back yards visible through the home. Most mildewed objects that had been hauled to the curbs have been picked up.

About 4 weeks after the storm, the surviving trees began to show signs of green leafage, indicating that most trees and shrubs should come back to their original grandness within a few years.

***

"My wife and dog left on Saturday, I left on Sunday and the house left on Monday." (Gene Street of Gulfport)
***

John & Jan Bunc lived on 648 Kome Street in a new brick home when the storm arrived. John is a Deputy Sheriff with Hancock County. The water began to rise up to the back deck about 10:30 a.m. and then gradually up the windows. Objects in the house began to float and they began to realize that this could get even worse. Jan began to fill her new purse with important items and John told her to put on some shoes, as there was broken glass all over the area. He threw her a shoe as it came floating by and then found another for her, which she refused, as "they did not match"!

They debated about going into the attic, but decided that this could be a mistake and then decided to swim to higher ground. When the water was at the top of the door jam, they swam out the door, over the six-foot fence and headed towards the northeast towards higher ground and safety. Wet and safe, they were O.K., but lost everything in their house.

Lessons Learned?

Many lessons have been learned since Katrina, and one can only hope they will be taken into consideration as new committees prepare for the next hurricane season or any other upcoming natural disaster.

One lesson that the Diamondhead Board of Directors quickly learned was that it did not have the security force for such a tragedy and the disaster manual needed to be revised. Diamondhead was also not prepared to become a refugee center.

The inability to communicate with each other and state and local governments was probably the worst problem following the storm and was possibly the cause of many deaths. Police could not radio each other after Katrina. The dilemma of not enough radios and how to get information to the stations must be solved before the next storm arrives.

Most of Mississippi first responder capabilities were inoperable during and immediately after the storm. The National Guard and first responders had to rely on face-to-face communication between emergency centers and the field because of the failures in backup power. First responders, National Guard and all public and state officials needed much better services than were available following Katrina. Satellite phones and radio were the only available communication for many days and most satellite phones soon went dead because they could not be recharged. Towers for satellite phones were using batteries for service, and they soon expired.

One fuel truck headed for a tower to replenish its generator was stopped at gunpoint and its fuel taken for other purposes. Another fuel truck was redirected by State Police to Gulfport Memorial to refuel their generators. Hard decisions had to be made as fuel was needed everywhere for everything.

Phone numbers were being changed at emergency centers; but service providers such as the National Guard had not been informed of the changes, and critical messages were not getting through. Pearl River County sustained good communication service because they had previously used grant funds to purchase an up-to-date mobile communications center.

Later, both FEMA and the Red Cross sent amateur radio operators to evacuation centers and county Emergency Operating Centers to help with communication; but the first few days, the critical days, the communication systems failed badly. It is hard to believe that a nation that can hear a beep from a robot on Mars could not hear a peep from thousands of its citizens. No act of man or nature should be permitted to isolate so many people in America for so long a time.

The public in general hampered rescue efforts in many ways. There were instances of people coming into Mississippi demanding military escorts. If this did not work for them, they tried deceiving the patrols by requesting help such as, "We have been hijacked," or "We ran out of gas on such and such Hwy." When help arrived, they would admit that they had just wanted an escort, which severely hampered emergency workers needed in other areas.

Those in the South saw first hand how the government failed to wisely utilize its resources and the taxpayer's money. The government wasted millions of dollars in its contracts for Katrina relief, many awarded with no-bids. Large companies were offered the contracts at very high prices and with no competition. Much was wasted. After future storms, private companies are going to be used for emergency supplies and other help according to Max Mayfield. Max is the director of the National Hurricane Center and is convinced that the government cannot do this job on its own. "Private enterprise has the experience and the resources and I am convinced this is the way to go in the future," said Max.

Hurricane Camille, which struck the Gulf Coast 36 years earlier, provided the opportunity to study and learn; but soon those lessons were forgotten. Camille was the hurricane of all hurricanes for the Coastal area. It was felt that if water did not reach a certain property during that storm, it never will in the future. That has been the guideline since 1969. However, Katrina proved this to be wrong. With the future predictions of global warming and ocean waters rising several feet in height, people must give a serious thought to reform and to building near the water. Residents did respect nature as an awesome force for a few years after

Camille, but soon all lessons were forgotten. The same lessons have once again been learned from Katrina. All communities need to research which programs should be initiated and which ones should be "ready to go" when the next big one approaches. Homes must be built according to stricter building code guidelines. New homes along the water must be stronger and safer and on higher elevations. Cities are considering using Smart Codes, which will make better communities.

People have short memories and the word "mandatory" in the years to come will mean only that first-responders will again need to do whatever it takes to get people out of harm's way. Climatologists warn that global warming will bring even harsher and stronger storms in this century. The Gulf Coast needs to be prepared.

Katrina has changed the South and it will never again be the same, but it can be better!

Kathleen Gremillion tells her story:

"Too exhausted from boarding windows to evacuate, we rode out the storm watching and praying for any Savior, be it God or the passage of time. Both of our elderly mothers were with us on the north side of Diamondhead. After the storm passed, a strange uneasy quiet enveloped us all, knowing that we had survived a major catastrophe dawned on us without benefit of any news media. Strangers passing on foot informed us of the water surge. Our inner turmoil would not allow us to face or discuss the possibility of family members not having made it through the storm.

A heat like none we have ever experienced settled down upon us and we realized that we could lose one of our mothers, as we were with-out water or electricity. We discussed repeatedly how many gallons of water we had on hand and how long could it last. We salvaged a few house screens that my mother mended with sewing thread to keep the relentless bugs at bay.

Looters were in the area so we dug out the gun and slept poorly from exhaustion and fear, always listening for cars coming into our cut de sac to do us harm.

Informing my mother-in-law that her house in the Oaks had flooded and that she had lost everything was like being stuck in a bad dream; yet we could not seem to wake up and shake it off.

There was no phone service and rumors flowed that if we were to leave, the National Guard would not allow us to return. Three days fol-lowing the storm seemed like years had passed. The sky was so black at night; it was as if we were the only people in the whole world. We had never felt such isolation and aloneness.

Soon our sisters arrived with supplies and evacuated the mothers. We then discussed the possibility of filling the old truck with our rations, using our siphoned gas, journey to New Orleans and help those poor people not one hour away. Rumors were that if we tried we would be turned back or harmed physically.

We heard horror stories as we waited in lines for water and MRE packaged meals. The bad "movie" we were stuck in was very surreal.

We decided to give up and leave, as all we could see was destruc-tion and hard work ahead for us. We could not count financial gain or loss as the value of everything we ever wanted was only a cool breeze or a piece of ice for our water. Now months have passed and we have evolved to a place that is still not certain, but we have changed the way we look at material things. We now value our neighbors, who were there for us when we needed them and realize that we cannot leave and aban-don what we have accomplished. We will remain?tomorrow, who knows?"

The End

The cleanup will take years, the rebuilding even longer, and South Mississippi, as it was prior to Katrina, will never be the same. However, people are attracted to the water, as bugs are to a light. They will return!

The suffering continues and will for years to come for those who lost loved ones or property in this terrible storm, the worst natural disaster in U.S. history.

Yet, the people hardest hit repeatedly say over and over again, "Thank you for the good old U.S.A. and the wonderful people who live in it; we would not be alive without you. You pulled us out of the rubble and gave us some hope."

As restaurants and businesses gradually open once again in "Katrina Land," we will soon forget that Katrina shut everything down, everything except the will of the people.

Those who felt the power of Katrina, no matter how slightly, will never forget her. "I will always become afraid when I hear the sound of a strong wind," stated a survivor.

"With so many trees going down in these tornados, many of us are now able to see the sunset, which we were unable to do so before Katrina", commented a Diamondhead resident.

Diamondhead will be Paradise Regained! (Chip Marz)

Today, the only thing that looks the same in South Mississippi is the Gulf of Mexico, some of which had to be the same water that battered the coast into oblivion during Katrina and now looks peaceful, gentle and passive. The sunsets are still spectacular and life will go on.

Sources

A number of sources were used to accumulate this work. References were found in the following:

Galveston and the 1900 Storm by Bixel and Turner, 2000, University of Texas Press

Category 5—The Story of Camille by Zebrowski and Howard, University of Michigan, Ann Arbor, Press

Hemingway's Hurricane, the Great Florida Keys Storm of 1935 by Phil Scott

All about Camille, by Dan Ellis

Information for the following comes from many, many articles that appeared in the Sun Herald, personal interviews with people who "rode out the storm" and those who later returned to witness the horrible mess Katrina had left. Times and figures come from documentation of the National Weather Service and emergency workers. Personal interviews were obtained from Diamondhead Manager Chip Marz, Chris Marz, Gene & Leona Wolfe, Mario Espanosa, Patricia Collier, Chief Westbrook and some of the fire crew, Dr. Patricia Collier from the Baptist Church, Linda Baur, Terre Settle, Joel Salzbury, Charles Corey, Betsey Nolan, Lady Anne Bruce, Jim & Lydia Jelinski, Steve Russell, Lynn Nelson, Joan Vaz, Mimi Pederson, Chuck Perry, Dot Schlafani, Mike Collard, Susan Necaise, John Bunc, Bill Dye, Shirley Smith, Bonita Favre, Elizabeth Sanderson, Al & Lou Revell, Scott Allgood and many more too numerous to mention.

Photos are by Linda Baur, Kathleen Gremillion, Lynn Tate, Lydia Jelinski, Darlene Courmier, Gene Wolfe, M.A. Welch, Jim Fagan, Maisie Condon, Marge Izydorek and author.

Endnotes

[1] Accu Weather Report done especially for Diamondhead by Joseph Sobel, Ph.D. and Stephen M. Wistar, Meterorlogists

[2] Interview with rescue personnel at the Fire Station

[3] Interview with Gene & Leona Wolfe

[4] Interview with JoAnn Vaz

[5] Interview with Mimi Pederson

[6] Interviews with Eugene & Leona Wolfe, Steve Russell, Mimi Pederson & Lynn Nelson

[7] Interview with Rescue people at Firehall and Anthony Sciacca

[8] Interview with Mario Espinosa

[9] Interview with Joel Salzbury

[10] *Sun Herald*, unknown date

[11] Interview with Mike Collard

[12] DVD by WLOX, *Katrina South Mississippi's Story*

[13] Interview with Tonya Perniciaro

[14] Interview with Dr. Patricia Collier

[15] Interview with Elizabeth Sanderson

[16] Interview with Dr. Patricia Collier

[17] Linda lived with the Plombons for about six months after the storm

[18] Interview with Shirley Smith

[19] Interview with Dot Schlafani

[20] Interview with the Jelinski

[21] *Sun Herald*

[22] Interview with Scott Allgood from the Edmond Fahey Funeral Home

[23] Hudsons is s well known discount store in the South

[24] Interview with Terre Settle

[25] Bonita Favre letter

[26] Interview with Susan Necaise

[27] *Leader Telegram (*Eau Claire, WI), 4 Sept, 2005

[28] Jimmie Brewer

[29] *Sun Herald*

[30] *Leader Telegram* (Eau Claire, WI), 4 Sept, 2005

[31] *Sun Herald*

[32] WLOX Special Report on Katrina

[33] Sun *Herald*

[34] *Sun Herald*

[35] Personal letter from Chip Marz, General Manager of POA

[36] Personal interview with Chuck Perry

[37] *Sun Herald*

[38] *Sun Herald,* Biloxi, MS

[39] Morrell Foundation website

[40] Interview with Bill Dye

Photo Descriptions

01. Friends and family helping the Jelinski family. (Photo by Jelinski)
02. What is left of home, yard and greenhouse of Tony and JoAnn Vaz (Photo by Izydorek)
03. Piles of household articles seen everywhere from gutting of homes. (Photo by Gremillion)
04. Cabinet holding good china remains intact on wall as other cabinets had been torn from wall. (Photo by Jelinski)
05. Life in a tent or FEMA trailer amidst the debris piles (Photo by Welch)
06. A few precious possessions pulled from the debris (Photo by Baur)
07. Gene Wolfe painfully relating his horrible experience delivered by Katrina (Photo by Baur)
08. First look at Linda Baur's living room after 6 feet of water. (Photo by Baur)
09. Taken by a cell phone, looking south from the bridge on the corner of Hwy 603 and I-10, shortly after the storm. Water was about 35 feet at this intersection and was now receding. (Photo by Tate)
10. About fifteen thousand Guardsmen from more than 40 states were seen about mid September in the area. (Photo by Baur)
11. Devastation as far as you can see and then miles after miles of it.(Photo by unknown)
12. Home of Joel Salzbury. (Photo by Baur)
13. Unusual items found in downtown Bay St. Louis. (Photo by Gremillion)
14. Some homes were not completely washed away on the south side of Diamondhead. (Photo by Baur)

15. All ditches around Diamondhead were found filled with strange items. (Photo by Author)

16. Destruction near beach. (Photo by Gremillion)

17. South side devastation. (photo by author)

18. Huge uprooted trees were everywhere. (Photo by Baur)

19. What is left of a lovely Southside backyard. Swimming pool in foreground and channel behind were filled with debris. (Photo by Baur)

20. Oaks photo (Photo by Gremillion)

21. The eye of Katrina

22. More treasures pulled from the debris. (Photo by Baur)

23. Thousands of pine trees were broken off 20-30 feet in air. (Photo by author)

24. Scene in Bay St. Louis, just behind the Fire Dog Saloon. Notice debris pushed into the car. (Photo by author)

25. Hundreds of semi trailers and huge industrial transport barges were tossed like toy trucks into homes and businesses. Vrazel's Restaurant sits among the rubble. (Photo by Gremillion)

26. The joy of cool water on a hot day at artesian well on north side of Diamondhead. The Jelinski family attempting to wash off black tar, which covered everything after the storm. (Photo by Jelinski)

27. The first Wal-Mart to open in a tent. Waveland. (Photo by Baur)

28. The Wolfe airplane, or what was left of it. (Photo by Wolfe)

29. Destruction on south side. Yacht Club in background, someone's home in foreground. (Photo by author)

30. Water rushing past the Baptist Church at Diamondhead during the storm. (Photo by Courmier)

31. A former Victorian mansion. (Photo by Gremillion)

32. East side homes collapse. (Photo by author)

33. Destruction as far as you can see in Waveland. (Photo by Gremillion)

34. Home of Bill Dye. (Photo by author)

35. Debris thrown into trees on south side of Diamondhead. (Photo by author)(Use on cover)

36. High water in Waveland. Taken during the storm. (Photo by Condon)

37. Typical scene of total desolation seen all along the coast.(Photo by Condon)

38. Diamondhead airport fuel tanker containing 10,000 gallons of fuel ripped from hangar and now blocking 3 lanes of I-10. (Photo unknown)

39. Biloxi beaches after the storm. (Photo by Gremillion)

40. Jim and Lydia Jelinski shortly after storm rehanging the family bell that disappeared during Katrina. (Photo by Jelinski)

41. Child's skis found amid debris on Southside. (Photo by author)

42. Yacht Club (Photo by Baur)

43. Shrimp boat rammed under a casino-parking ramp. One fisherman died in this boat. (Photo by Gremillion)

44. Water rising fast in the Oaks as seen through the rain and a window. (Photo by Baur)

45. Blue tarps were seen everywhere as most Diamondhead homes had some roof damage. (Photo by Fagan)

46. Only water available after storm on south side of Diamondhead flowing from artesian well. (Photo by Jelinski)

47. Unloading water and ice in shopping center at Diamondhead. (Photo by Baur)

48. Party dresses swinging in the breeze on hangars in destroyed east-side Diamondhead home. (Photo by Baur)

49. Cars in ditches along 603. Many have been removed and the road has been cleared. (Photo by Gremillion)

50. A spot of blue, high in the air was the welcoming scene for the Jelinski family. The house was standing, but badly damaged.(Photo by Jelinski)

51. Waveland devastation. (Photo by unknown)

52. Jelinski family walking in to check their property at dusk on Tuesday morning. (Photo by Jelinski)

53. The Jelinski back yard as viewed from the second floor of home. Note Lydia's grand piano on ground, washed out of the house and tumbled to ground. (Photo by Jelinski)

Index

About The Author

After gathering notes and personal stories from Katrina survivors and newspapers the author decided that this material should be shared with the public and to publish it as a book.

After raising five children she has fulfilled her days with volunteer work for local, county and state historical and genealogical societies. She retired from President of the Chippewa County Genealogical Society after 17 years of service including acting as newsletter editor. She helped raise that society from an infant to a very successful organization with a wonderful research library. She is currently museum director and newsletter editor of her local Stanley, Wisconsin, historical society and serves on the board of directors for the Chippewa County Historical Society.

She has made seventeen trips to Salt Lake City, attending week-long classes while there and doing research on her family lines and for other people.

Betty has compiled several local historical books and is currently writing six family history books.

She is a native of Stanley, Wisconsin, but now resides in Diamondhead, Mississippi. She and her husband, Bill, a retired funeral director, return to Stanley each summer. She loves to read, garden and to play golf and bridge.

Quick Order Form

Mail to Betty Plombon, 7725 Mamalu PL., Diamondhead, MS, 39525

Please send the following books

_____Colored books at $29.95 a book. Total cost $_____

_____Black & white books at $19.95 a book. Total cost $_____

Sales tax: Please add 7% if mailed to a MS address $_____
($2.09 per each colored book & $1.39 each per black and white)

Shipping U.S.: $4 for first book and $2 per each additional book $_____

Total cost included $_____

Name:_____

Address:_____

City, State & Zip_____

Quick Order Form

Mail to Betty Plombon, 7725 Mamalu PL., Diamondhead, MS, 39525

Please send the following books

_____Colored books at $29.95 a book. Total cost $_____

_____Black & white books at $19.95 a book. Total cost $_____

Sales tax: Please add 7% if mailed to a MS address $_____
($2.09 per each colored book & $1.39 each per black and white)

Shipping U.S.: $4 for first book and $2 per each additional book $_____

Total cost included $_____

Name:_____

Address:_____

City, State & Zip_____

Printed in the United States
76576LV00004B/151-186

9 781598 582208